DATE			
MAY 2 8 1986			
MAN 2 1 1987			
MAR 05 2014			

Psychology
Misdirected

Psychology Misdirected

Seymour B. Sarason

THE FREE PRESS
A Division of Macmillan Publishing Co., Inc.
NEW YORK

Collier Macmillan Publishers
LONDON

The Free Press
A Division of Macmillan Publishing Co., Inc.
866 Third Avenue, New York, N.Y. 10022

Collier Macmillan Canada, Ltd.

Library of Congress Catalog Card Number: 80-69283

Printed in the United States of America

1 2 3 4 5 6 7 8 9 10

Library of Congress Cataloging in Publication Data

Sarason, Seymour Bernard
　　Psychology misdirected.

　　Bibliography: p.
　　Includes index.
　　1. Psychology—Philosophy. 2. Psychology—
Social aspects. 3. Psychology—United States—
History. I. Title. [DNLM: 1. Psychology, Social.
HM291 S243p]
BF38.S227　　　150.1　　　80-69283
ISBN 0-02-928100-8　　　AACR2

To
John Dewey
Prophet with Honor

CONTENTS

PREFACE

I had to overcome a good deal of resistance to write this book because what I have to say is very critical of psychology and of the social sciences generally. To be critical of one part of a highly complex and differentiated field like psychology is one thing, but to take the position that the entire discipline is seriously misdirected is quite another. But I concluded finally that there was too much at stake to justify silence. Crucial to the decision to write this book was the conclusion, based on a good deal of experience and observation, that many psychologists (and other social scientists) are disenchanted with and disaffected from the field but, for understandable reasons, have difficulty publicly stating their feelings. We define ourselves, and society defines us, largely in terms of what we do, our work, and if we come to have serious doubts about the underpinnings, thrust, social meanings and uses of our endeavors we tend to still those doubts with a variety of stratagems that permit us to keep going, albeit with an undercurrent of dysphoria. If I felt that this was the case for a very small number of psychologists I would not have felt justified in writing this book. But my experience has taught me it is true for an undetermined but significant number of psychologists.

This book has several major themes. First, psychology at its core has been quintessentially a study of the individual organism unrelated to the history, structure, and unverbalized world views of the social order. Second, psychologists have never been a random sample of the population in terms of their niche in and influence on the social order, a fact that, together with their inability to confront the nature of the social order, has permitted them wrongly to assume that their theories and practices are *substantively* independent of their relationship to the social order. Third, the limitations suggested by the first two themes could not become apparent as long as psychology was largely a university based, laboratory oriented discipline devoted to exploring and mapping the fundamentals of "human nature." But World War II changed psychology, as it changed everything else, and psychology eagerly and willingly entered the public arena in heretofore undreamed of ways. Optimism is the word that best describes the outlook of psychologists in the two decades after World War II. Malaise and confusion are appropriate words to describe the outlook of many psychologists today. How does one explain this dramatic change, a change by no means peculiar to psychologists?

The answer is, of course, terribly complex but one part of it, I argue, derives from dependence on an asocial individual psychology content to ignore the fact that psychologists, no less than those they studied and about whom they theorized, were and are products of a socialization process from which they absorbed a particular view of people and society. This view inevitably is contained in psychological theories which are pictures of people and the social order. And these pictures are pitifully inadequate as a representation of the real world. In some ultimate sense it would be sad but not catastrophic for society if psychology did not live up to its earlier promise. Unfortunately, a case can be made that by virtue of its constricted focus and failure to see its derivation from and relationship to the social order, psychology has adversely affected the lives of many people. Psychologists have always assumed, and their professional organizations have proclaimed, an identity between the discipline's needs and aims and those of the social order. In practice this has meant that psychology serves the social order, a stance that exposes how well psychology has been socialized into the social order, thereby rendering it unable to take distance from it. I do not suggest that psychology should automatically assume an adversarial stance but I do assert that the assumption of an identity of needs and interests is ultimately self-defeating. The promise of psychology will be reformulated, and the current malaise overcome only if the discipline begins to see that it inevitably plays a cause and effect role in the social order. Psychology put itself on the course of affecting the social order without examining how that social order caused the substance and practices of psychology. That social order became part of the substance of psychological theory no less effectively than the air we breathe enters our bloodstream. Just as we have learned that the air we breathe may be inimical to our health, psychology has to learn that the social order from which it derives and with which it has a symbiotic relationship may contain features inimical to its health. But that kind of learning, however, requires that psychologists begin to transcend, if only in part, their socialization into the social order.

I consider this book applicable to all fields of psychology if only because every psychologist embeds his or her particular interest in a picture that describes what people and the social world are like. A psychologist may have no interest whatsoever in changing people or the world, and just wants to be left alone to pursue his or her interests. The fact is that that psychologist has a picture of what people are and can be, a picture into which, explicitly or implicitly, these interests are put. That psychologist may not feel it necessary to explicate that picture or to examine its derivation, but that is no warrant for overlooking the central issue in psychology; the ways in which the psychologist's socialization and place in the social order become part of the picture, part of the substance of theory. Psychologists theorize about people, and they start with pictures of what people are or can be. They do not dream up these pictures. The socialization process is intended to give one a picture of man and society; it does not encourage inquiry into that picture. Some people never feel a need to question the picture; some question it in restricted ways; a few reject it and begin to paint another picture. Psychology has had very few of the last group and it is not happenstance that they have been either ignored or read out of the field. John Dewey was one such person and that is why I devote a chapter to his 1899 presidential address to the American Psychological Association in New Haven. "Psychology and Social Practice" is the most atypical and seminal address ever given to that association, but neither then nor now has psychology comprehended what Dewey had to say. His view of man and society, of psychology in relation to the social order, could not be more challenging to and different from the narrow, superficial pictures of the psychological establishment, and it was easiest to discuss Dewey by calling him an educator and a philosopher.

It will be apparent to the knowledgeable reader that I have been influenced by (and borrowed from) many more people than I mention in this book. I did not feel called upon to justify my opinions by citing those of others. I make no pretense that this book is other than an attempt through a series of related essays to examine the same issues from somewhat different perspectives or contexts. Candor requires that I say that I would regard any criticism of this book that is based on the belief that psychology is alive and well, or that psychology is sick but the corrective medicine has been found and health is just a matter of time, to be egregiously Panglossian. And I would be no less disappointed if this book were praised because it purports to ask psychologists to look into themselves. Of course the thrust of my argument is that psychologists have to *re*view themselves but from the special standpoint of how their society is organized, how it works, how it socializes different groups in different ways, and how it specifically has influenced the theories and practices of psychologists. If I intended to emphasize anything in this book it is how ahistorical, ignorant, and naive psychologists have been about their society and how it is reflected in them. In underlining the severe limitations of an asocial, individual psychology, I am in no way suggesting that such an emphasis has been sterile. Psychology has contributed to our understanding of human behavior and to suggest otherwise is at best nonsense and at worst an indulgence of nihilism. But we have paid a price for this approach in that is has obscured the implications of the fact that American psychology, invented in and by American society, went on to invent its subject matter, the self-contained individual. The necessity for reinvention is urgent.

Initially, this book was to be part of a larger work that would be autobiographical in nature, not because the world needs or wants my autobiography but because that genre would permit me in a concrete and personal way to illustrate themes and concepts that somehow lose force when handled more abstractly. I have been told by my students that it is not until I use my own experience to make a point that they can identify something in their lives with that experience. This is particularly the case when I am trying to get them to see how much of history is in the present, unrecognized and unverbalized. But the autobiography got derailed in the course of preparing a keynote address for the Fourth Vermont Conference on the Primary Prevention of Psychopathology. Preparing that paper (Sarason, 1980) convinced me that psychology's unreflective dependence on a theory of the individual organism required a separate effort. Besides, the arrogance implied in writing an autobiography continued to present a problem to me.

Several colleagues and friends have been in ways known and unknown to them extraordinarily helpful to me in thinking through this book. It is, therefore, a real pleasure to express my gratitude to them for listening and reacting to my ramblings, for letting me listen to their ramblings, and for the comfort of their intellectual and personal friendship. I refer specifically to Wendell Garner, Thomas Gladwin, Louis Heifetz, and Michael Klaber. Marlene Twarowski came along just when this manuscript needed final typing and her competence and graciousness contributed enormously to my mental health.

One writes for many reasons and for different people, and in this instance, as it has always been for me, at the top of the list are Esther and Julie Sarason.

SEYMOUR B. SARASON
New Haven, Connecticut

CHAPTER I

THE SOCIAL SCIENCES
IN DISARRAY

IT IS HARD TO EXAGGERATE THE DIFFERENCE in climate and outlook in
the social sciences between today and two decades ago. For a short
period after World War II the social sciences experienced remarkable
growth in terms of numbers, funding, prestige, and influence in the
halls of public and private power. Social scientists were cocky and con-
fident, led by economists who said they knew how to fine tune the
economy to avoid recessions, followed by sociologists enamored with
grand, abstract theories of the structure and dynamics of society, and
not far behind were psychologists promising much about their capacity
to fathom the basic laws of development and behavior, to prevent individual abnormalities and misery, and to repair the insidious, self-
defeating consequences of neurosis. Anthropologists, who became in-
stantly valuable to the government during World War II, became even
more so with the war's end, when the nation emerged as the dominant
military-social-political force in the world and took on administrative
supervision of diverse peoples and cultures. Before World War II the
social sciences were, except for economics, university based disciplines
having, for all practical purposes, no ties with the political system.
World War II changed all that; social scientists became needed and
they wanted to be needed. They envied the status and support the
natural sciences had gained by virtue of contributions to the war effort
and the vistas those contributions opened for future "progress." The

1

time had come, the social scientists argued, for our society to recognize that unless it took the lead to strengthen and support the social sciences we would miss a golden (and perhaps final) opportunity to gain that kind of knowledge and understanding necessary to reshape the social order, national and international, and to contain and even eliminate the destructive forces that had brought about World War II.

Growth in the social sciences had other stimuli, the two most important of which were the GI bill, which brought millions of veterans into colleges and universities, and the perceived population explosion, for which the facilities in higher education would be grossly inadequate. But it was not simply that many more highly trained social scientists would be needed in the universtiy. The fact was that many of the students who began pouring into colleges and universities were, like their social science teachers, imbued with the desire to build a new and better world. They wanted answers and direction no less than the social scientists sought to provide them with answers and direction. World War II had upset the old order and it seemed obvious that to build a new and more healthy order required a vigorous, bold, imaginative, socially responsive social science. No one was naive enough to claim that the task would be easy and that mistakes would not be made. But there was consensus about several things: the research endeavor was the only way in which a solid base for social construction could be developed; the research endeavor must derive from clear, formal theory that produced testable hypotheses; and at all stages of the theory-research process quantification was both means and end, i.e., it was the way of discovering and testing new relationships and it was a step preliminary to the mathematization of variables and forces.*

After World War II the emphasis on, indeed the preoccupation with, theory-research-quantification put a distinctive mark on American social science. What is a theory? What are the differences between a good and a bad theory? What are or should be the relationships among axioms, the formal characteristics of a theory, and hypotheses? These and other questions reflected an agonizing self-consciousness centering around the belief that if social science were

---

*This was not an unfamiliar stance in psychology. In the thirties Clark Hull and Kurt Lewin, two very different kinds of psychologists, had sought to wed psychology to mathematics and formal logic. Hull developed a mathematico-deductive theory of rote learning, and Lewin used topological geometry in his theory of personality organization.

truly to be science, it had to learn from and emulate natural science. It was recognized, of course, that natural and social science had different subject matters but that made it all the more important for "soft" social science to understand how natural science had become "hard": to become hard meant rigorous theory building, experimental research, and sophisticated statistical-mathematical analysis.

There was an intimate connection between this conception of hardness and optimism about the future. To the degree that social science was now on the right path one was justified in being optimistic. But there was more to the optimism than that. The United States had emerged from World War II as a colossus—militarily, economically, politically, and psychologically. When I say "psychologically" I mean from two perspectives, the American and that of the rest of the world. The United States citizen saw his country as the cultural and economic savior of a war ravaged world. In World War I *we* had "saved" the world from the ambitions of the German kaiser, and *we* repeated that feat in World War II against a far more destructive, fascist-racist foe. With the end of World War II it seemed that the primary responsibility for building a new world—*not* rebuilding it on the old basis—was *ours*. Just as Copernicus had put the sun at the center of the universe, World War II had placed the United States at the center of the earth's social world. This perspective was shared "psychologically" by peoples in countries that saw the United States as the most powerful force in the world. These countries were magnetically attracted to this force, seeing in it a way of insuring their future and freedom (variously defined). There were other countries (e.g., Russia, China) that understood this magnetism but were fearful of what it could mean for the societies they wished to build.

Like the bulk of the United States citizenry, social scientists shared this view of the country's place and responsibility in the world, a view that undergirded their optimism about what their fields could contribute to a better world. But unlike most citizens, social scientists recognized that the task was not simply one of exporting resources and ideology; rather, there were social problems internal to the country that had to be confronted. This recognition, however, only made the overall task more complex; it did not dim the optimism about the outcome.

As one goes back over the history of the two decades after World War II, one might conclude that the optimism of the social scientist was diagnostic of faulty reality testing. Hardly a week went by when nationally or internationally there was not an event or crisis that signaled the presence of long-standing conflicts. Instability rather than stability characterized the world order. And within the country there did not seem to be much basis for optimism either. Racial conflicts and riots, the emerging civil rights movement, escalating juvenile delinquency, economic recessions and dislocations, Senator Joseph McCarthy's witch hunts, the Korean war, labor-management struggles, urban decay—these were only some of the things that were socially unsettling and seemed intractable. Why, then, the optimism of the social scientist? The answer to this question has three parts.

The first involves the degree to which social science believed that scientifically attained, so-called hard knowledge had an inexorable quality that society could neither resist nor avoid. The assumption was that society needed *and* wanted that knowledge, which, when forthcoming, would help transform the social order. It is as though social science operated on the maxim that "knowledge will set you free," not realizing that the maxim might be true for individuals (the "you") but not for a social order.

The second part of the answer is that society, in the form of the federal government, was willing materially to support the efforts of social science to attain the hard knowledge. For the first time social science saw itself as needed and wanted by a respectful society; that is, by virtue of the support, society was agreeing with the social scientists that the knowledge they would provide would be as influential as the contributions of the natural sciences. That kind of support and respect was heady stuff and not calculated to dampen optimism about the potential of social science.

The third part of the answer is more complex and in subtle ways derives from the first two parts. The identification with hard science (the preoccupation with theory building, research, and mathematization) and the willing dependence of social science on government support short-circuited any tendency to focus on the underlying, usually unverbalized, unreflectively assimilated assumptions, axioms, and values of the social order. It is perhaps more correct to say that like everyone else the social scientist had been socialized to the culture and society and as a consequence had a view of himself or herself, of the society, and of the world that was distinctive, indeed unique. To be born and reared in the United States gave one a world view that was not the same as if one had been born and reared in Canada, or Mexico, or England, or Russia, or an African colony. This may not be as severe a problem for the natural scientist in relation to his subject matter, but for the social scientist intent on understanding and contributing to the alteration of the social order into which he has been socialized, it is a mammoth and (should be) an unavoidable problem. But American social science after World War II managed, as it did before that war, to skirt the problem.

There were, and always had been, social scientists who saw the problem clearly and were able, in varying degrees, to flush out and analyze the underlying picture of society and man upon which our capitalist society is based, a picture that includes an impersonal market economy, competition between individuals and between firms, acceptance of individual self-interest as a fact of life (if not of human nature), and the accumulation of material resources as a desirable goal. Thorstein Veblen and Albion Small are two social scientists from earlier in this century who come to mind; others came after them. Small poignantly saw that the future of the new science of sociology would be a social disaster if the discipline took on the trappings of science at the same time that it lost sight of the nature of the society from which this new science emerged and for which it was to be a force for change. Small was not anti-science: he accepted wholeheartedly the traditions and public morality of science, but he also knew that these traditions and morality could be subverted and rendered trivial and impotent by sociologists who blithely accepted the social order, especially if that meant that sociology would gain respect as a hard science. Becker (1971), in *The Lost Science of Man,* views Small as a tragic figure precisely because Small helped produce what he so earnestly wanted to avoid. Veblen is another story. That we live in a capitalist society was obvious enough to him, nor was that society as a system the object of his analysis or criticism. What Veblen was after was the relationship between wealth and behavior, i.e., the consequences of wealth on those who possess and therefore on those who lack it. In his preface to Veblen's *Theory of the Leisure Class,* Galbraith (1973) states well and tartly Veblen's accomplishment:

> The book is a truly devastating put-down, as it would now be called. But much more was involved. The *Theory of the Leisure Class* brilliantly and truthfully illuminates the effect of wealth on behavior. No one who has

read this book ever again sees the consumption of goods in the same light. Above a certain level of affluence the enjoyment of goods—of dress, houses, automobiles, entertainment—can never again be thought intrinsic as, in a naive way, the established or neoclassical economics still holds it to be. Possession and consumption are the banner which advertises achievement—which proclaims, by the accepted standards of the community, that the possessor is a success. In this sense—in revealing what had not hitherto been seen—the *Theory of the Leisure Class* is a major scientific achievement. . . .

In fact Veblen's anthropology and sociology are weapon and armor rather than science. He uses them to illuminate (and to make ridiculous) the behavior of the most powerful class—the all-powerful class—of his time. And since he does it in the name of science and with the weapons of science—and since no overt trace of animus or anger is allowed to appear—he does it with nearly perfect safety. The butterfly does not attack the zoologist for saying that it is more decorative than useful. That Marx was an enemy whose venom was to be returned in kind, capitalists did not doubt. But not Veblen. The American rich never quite understood what he was about—or what he was doing to them. The scientific pretense, the irony and the careful explanations that the most pejorative words were being used in a strictly nonpejorative sense put him well beyond their comprehension. (Pp. xvii– xviii)

I cannot refrain from quoting once more from Galbraith's preface:

The last chapter of *The Leisure Class* is on "The Higher Learning as an Expression of the Pecuniary Culture." It anticipates a later, much longer and much more pungent disquisition by Veblen on the influence of the pecuniary civilization on the university. In this chapter Veblen—though also concerned with other matters—stresses the conservative and protective role of the universities in relation to the pecuniary culture. "New views, new departures in scientific theory, especially new departures which touch the theory of human relations at any point, have found a place in the scheme of the university tardily and by a reluctant tolerance, rather than by cordial welcome; and the men who have occupied themselves with such efforts to widen the scope of human knowledge have not commonly been well received by their learned contemporaries." No one will be in doubt as to whom, in the last clause, Veblen had in mind. Elsewhere he notes that "As further evidence of the close relation between the educational system and the cultural standards of the community, it may be remarked that there is some tendency latterly to substitute the captain of industry in place of the priest, as head of seminaries of the higher learning." (P. xix)

I have long been puzzled by the reluctance of social scientists to characterize their society as capitalistic. Indeed, I feel it is less a reluctance than a sense that such a characterization would be an admission of unseemly features in the society. Granted that one can generate quite a controversy about a definition of capitalism as an ideology and an economic system, or about the validity of Karl Marx's account of the past, present, and future of capitalism, the fact remains that we live in a society organized around a market economy, associated and suffused with competitivenes, underlying which is an individual psychology that takes for granted the benefits of achievement motivation, "success," and the garnering of material wealth. Nor can it be denied that some of the most unseemly aspects of our national history have resulted from these characteristics; the same is true of our international impact. It is not to indulge paradox to point out that the pages of this same history also contain some of man's most wondrous achievements, not the least of which have centered around the defense of human freedom and dignity. But if ours is a society replete with contradictions, an amalgam of the good and the bad, containing conflicts and inequities as defined by our own tradition and rhetoric, we cannot be gun-shy about a label like "capitalism," which requires us to come to grips with the discrepancies between what rhetoric says we are and social practice says we are not, between the benefits our society confers and the price we pay for them, between the opportunities available for individual expression and the miseries of loneliness, between the guarantees of equal opportunity and the facts of discrimination.

In terms of outlook and concerns people like Veblen and Small (and more recently C. Wright Mills, Alvin Gouldner, and J. F. Brown) have always been in a small minority in American social science.* Mainstream social science, represented and institutionalized in the university, has managed to avoid the problem the work of this minority poses: how can the social scientist understand the very society

---

*Mills, Gouldner, and Brown have in common an orientation, a basic assumption of which is that the theories of social scientists are highly related to where they are in the social order. They also inveigh against social science because of its failure to confront that relationship in theory and practice. Much that is in Mills's (1959) *Sociological Imagination,* Gouldner's (1970) *Coming Crisis of Western Sociology,* and Brown's (1936) *Psychology and the Social Order* influenced my thinking. Most readers will be unfamiliar with J. F. Brown, a psychologist who wrote in the thirties and was massively ignored. I discuss his writing later in this book.

into which the social scientist was born and reared? Asked in this way the answer is unfortunately clear: the social scientist's understanding will at best have a tunnel-vision quality that focuses elsewhere than on the unverbalized assumptions and world view on which the society is based, even though that person seeks to see things whole and to get below the social surface. At worst, the social scientist will be mindlessly occupied with trivia, smugly unaware of any problem other than the one "out there." The significance of the small minority of any period is that they are able, for reasons by no means clear, to resist and question their own socialization.

Far from recognizing the problems inherent in understanding the society into which one has been socialized, and far from confronting directly the underlying assumptions of capitalist society, social scientists in the immediate post–World War II period turned outward rather than inward; that is to say, they became preoccupied with formal theory building (there seemed to be as many "models" or "paradigms" as in the world of fashion), method, and quantitative analysis. The enthusiasm with which they greeted the advent of the age of computers was but one instance of how social science had absorbed the science-technology view of its subject matter. I trust that the reader will not interpret what I have just said as a criticism of science, theory, research, or computers. What I am suggesting is that the unbridled eagerness with which social science took on all the trappings of what it thought was hard science inhibited the pursuit of the bedeviling issues surrounding the following question: to what extent and in what ways was social science uncritically accommodating to the dominant outlook of the society, i.e., to an outlook that defined not only what was a legitimate problem but also what were the ways such problems should be attacked. Put in another way: was there not a real cause for concern when social science found itself in basic agreement with the ways in which the society (in the form of federal policy and support) was defining problems and solutions?

Let me illustrate what I mean by a public policy that was initiated soon after World War II, a policy greeted with approval and happy fantasies by almost everyone, including social scientists. I refer to the decision to carpet the country with interstate highways. I daresay that there was no social scientist who was not enamored of the possibility of driving from coast to coast without ever having to stop for a red light. Pulling off such an engineering feat would be as American as apple pie, and no less satisfying to our appetites. But a public policy rarely, if ever, gets formulated and implemented because of abstract conceptions of virtue, although it may be promoted on that basis. Although a policy has to be seen as consistent with the society's traditions and picture of the public welfare, its adoption (or rejection) always reflects (in our society) the activities of competing self-interest groups varying in political and economic power. Public policy is forged in a marketplace of power and influence, and if you are not in that marketplace your future and self-interests are determined by others. What was unusual about the initial highway policy was that it seemed to enjoy almost unanimous public support and played to the self-interests of diverse groups (e.g., the military, truckers, the oil industry, car manufacturers, the concrete and steel industry). One might have expected that social scientists would have shown a serious interest in the policy because of the changes and dislocations it could produce, e.g., on people living in ghettos that would be wiped out, on the social and economic health of cities, on people who would leave the city for suburban living, on the railroad system, and on family organization and life. What adverse trends discernible in the society's past would be accelerated by the policy? In light of the groups that stood to gain the most economically by the policy, should one not look into the human and social "losses" that would more than offset the "profits" of these groups? Given a society that by its economic structure and dynamics, as well as by its emphasis on individualism and by the obstacles it raised to the maintenance of a sense of community, why should one look with pride on a policy that could exacerbate feelings of rootlessness? A very good case could be made that the highway policy had a greater and more harmful effect on people's sense of belonging and well-being than any other single policy adopted in the post–World War II era.

It is not that the policy was capricious or mindless; nor was it in any way a conspiracy by special-interest groups to foist something on the citizenry. The policy had its root in two beliefs (among others): economic growth is necessary and good, and whatever contributes to economic growth contributes to individual well-being. In short, *that* is progress and how can one be against progress? These beliefs were part of the basis for the policies we adopted in our efforts to help "underdeveloped" countries, i.e., to make their societies like ours, to substitute our beliefs for theirs, to take them off the road of primitivism and direct them on the road to progress.

None of the social sciences was at all alert in the early post–World

War II period to the significance of the highway policy. As I relive those days I am struck by the number of social scientists I knew who could not wait to enjoy the benefits of fast, efficient, transcontinental travel. They seemed not at all self-conscious about the fact that *they* belonged to those strata in society that could take maximum advantage of the system. The significance of differential use of a highway system that would cost billions of dollars (a good deal of which would come from gasoline taxes on people who would use the system least and whose homes would be razed for highway construction) did not enter social science thinking. Social scientists, like almost everyone else, had been too effectively socialized to resist the lures and imagined benefits of technology, bold engineering, and economic growth.* It took two decades or so for some social scientists to begin to see that by virtue of their socialization certain questions simply could not enter their minds and that there were features to the society they had not wanted to face or whose significance they had grossly underestimated.

Optimism propels one to the future. When it turns out that the optimism was unjustified it is frequently the case that the false optimism was in part a consequence of the neglect of social history. In *The Creation of Settings and the Future Societies* (1972), I describe at some length how in the post–World War II era many unsuccessful efforts at institutional innovation and change were characterized by an uncritical optimism that blinded people to how much of the past existed in their present. Optimism is a double-edged sword: it can have adaptive and creative consequences, but it can also reinforce an ahistorical stance that defeats one's purposes.

The social sciences have not been noted for their historical perspective. Indeed, after World War II, the social sciences seemed far more interested in the history of hard science than in that of their own fields. (The *nouveaux riches* downplay or flee from their backgrounds.) But

*Other societies, other views. About ten years ago the Norwegians found oil under their seas. Far from having visions of a bountiful future, Norwegian leaders reacted with a kind of fear. What could happen to their society if they plunged into the development of the oil fields and began to collect billions of dollars from the sale of the oil? What would be the consequences for Norwegian culture, for their sense of continuity with their past, for their sense of community? A decision was made to go as slowly as possible, to give priority to what they regarded as the important issue in living. The Norwegians know that they live in a world they cannot control, that they will be subject to pressures within and without their society to develop the oil fields quickly and fully. They may not be able to have it their way. But *their* way in regard to oil is in startling contrast to our way in regard to thousands of miles of concrete ribbons.

there were, as always, a few social scientists who did not fit the mold that was being forged in those postwar days. One of them was Robert Nisbet and among his many splendid books *The Quest for Community* is most relevant for my present purposes because of when it was written, the dominant themes it contains, and the demonstration that social history is not a museum of relics to be viewed on the Sundays of our lives as respite from an unpleasant world. The book germinated in Nisbet's mind in the forties and was published in 1953. In the 1971 preface of a new printing Nisbet (1971b) explains why he had not made changes in the book:

I believe today, as I believed throughout the 1940's, when this book was beginning to take form in my mind, that the single most impressive fact in the twentieth century in Western society is the fateful combination of widespread quest for community—in whatever form, moral, social, political—and the apparatus of political power that has become so vast in contemporary democratic states. That combination of search for community and existing political power seems to me today, just as it did twenty years ago, a very dangerous combination. For, as I argue in this book, the expansion of power feeds on the quest for community. All too often, power comes to resemble community, especially in times of convulsive social change and of widespread preoccupation with personal identity, moral certainty, and social meaning. This is, as I try to make clear throughout the book, the essential tragedy of modern man's quest for community. Too often the quest has been through channels of power and revolution which have proved destructive of the prime sources of human community. The structure of political power which came into being three centuries ago on the basis of its eradication of medieval forms of community has remained—has indeed become ever more—destructive of the contexts of new forms of community. (Pp. vii–viii).

Nisbet goes on to say that if he were to make changes they would involve greater emphasis on certain themes. One of these themes is alienation:

I would, I think, give it even greater importance in the book today than I did when I wrote it twenty years ago, well before the contemporary deluge of books and articles on alienation had begun. For it has become steadily clearer to me that alienation is one of the determining realities of the contemporary age. It will not do to relegate it to the realm of the symbols which influence intellectuals and which do not, at first thought, seem to implicate the lives of others in society. In the first place, intellectuals' symbols, taken as a whole, widely and often deeply influence popular behavior. For we live in an age of rather high literacy. And in the second place the same currents of thought and feeling which have caught up intellectuals have also, in different ways, at different levels, caught up large numbers of persons who do not pretend to be intellectuals but who are responsive nonetheless to the urgencies of the time. For many of them, too, alienation is a conspicuous state of mind.

By alienation I mean the state of mind that can find a social order remote, incomprehensible, or fraudulent; beyond real hope or desire; inviting apathy, boredom, or even hostility. The individual not only does not feel a part of the social order; he has lost interest in being a part of it. For a constantly enlarging number of persons, including, significantly, young persons of high school and college age, this state of alienation has become profoundly influential in both behavior and thought. Not all the manufactured symbols of togetherness, the ever-ready programs of human relations, patio festivals in suburbia, and our quadrennial crusades for presidential candidates hide the fact that for millions of persons such institutions as state, political party, business, church, labor union, and even family have become remote and increasingly difficult to give any part of one's self to.

There is another way of noting this: through the prevailing reactions of intellectuals to social and economic issues; Schumpeter, in his great book *Capitalism, Socialism and Democracy,* wrote that one of the flaws of capitalism is its inexhaustible capacity for alienating the intellectuals. This is true, but it needs qualification. For a long time capitalism at least supplied the motive power for revolt among intellectuals. This was not only an important manifestation of social energy but also a subtle form of identification. (No one revolts against what he is totally alienated from.) I am thinking of such matters as the struggle for the rights of the underprivileged, labor unions, ethnic equality, and the like. But it is hard to miss the fact that today there is a kind of alienation even from the ideological issues of capitalism, leading one to wonder what is to supply the friction in the future for social change. (Pp. viii–x)

I shall make no attempt to summarize Nisbet's book. More important for my purposes than its different themes and its illumination of social and intellectual history is Nisbet's artistry in showing us how as individuals we are stamped by time, place, culture, and history, a stamp that we ordinarily are unaware of and that pushes us in directions that, however understandable, dialectically produce the opposite of that for which we yearn. So, when one reads Nisbet's book and then looks back at the highway policy that intrigued so many people, one understands better how the political-economic features of a particular society can blind its people to how these features may exacerbate their feelings of alienation.*

Although Nisbet is an eminent and highly respected sociologist–social historian, he has not been a mainstream social scientist. Unlike most social scientists who following World War II were more interested in the history of science than in the history of their society, who were more interested in the "hardness" of their discipline than in the hardness of their society, who sought and related to those in seats of power rather than questioning why and how they were permitting themselves to be used with what consequences, who were far more analytic about the nature of formal theory than about the formal nature of the society, who confused change with progress and fact with knowledge—unlike those in mainstream social science, Nisbet has that rare capacity to take distance from, to seek to unimprison himself from, the consequences of his socialization. Whereas it took a couple of decades for social scientists generally to begin to become aware of the unintended consequences of the directions they had taken, those same unintended consequences were forecasted in Nisbet's writings.

Today the social sciences are in disarray. One would not know this from reading the literature because it continues to have the same characteristics it took on after World War II.† But one would know it

*There is a final significance to Nisbet's book for my purposes: the current malaise in the social sciences, their disillusionment about themselves and society's disenchantment with them, the alienation of many social scientists from their fields and sometimes from their work, *their* lack of a sense of community—all of these features were implied and in general forecasted in Nisbet's analysis written in the heyday of optimism. The uncritical and unreflective manner in which academia made itself available to and dependent on the federal government and the adverse consequences this had on the structure of and relationships within the university are described by Nisbet in *The Degradation of the Academic Dogma* (1971a). In light of what I shall be saying in later pages about John Dewey, particularly the issues he raised about the psychologist's "political conditioning," I find it pleasantly ironic that this later book by Nisbet consists of an elaboration on a series of lectures to the John Dewey Society.

†In psychology a few people (not fortuitously, social psychologists) have articulated their belief that psychology has been misdirected. Gergen (1973, 1976, 1978, 1979a, b), whose work I cite in the next chapter, has analyzed the sources of this misdirection in a series of instructive, scholarly papers. Berkowitz (1970), Brewster Smith (1973), and Katz (1972) have also published misgivings. Two papers by Proshansky (1972, 1978) contain a searing indictment of psychology's course.

from talking privately with social scientists. They will admit that
something is (and went) wrong, that the promise of social science has
not paid off; that the world of affairs does not conform to social science
models and paradigms; that there is a massive gulf between knowledge
and purposes, on the one hand, and actions appropriate to them, on
the other hand; that the more you try to change things the more they
seem to remain the same; that perhaps the natural science conception
of solutions is not applicable to social problems; that the "patron-
artist" relationship between social science and central government has
been a very mixed blessing, a relationship far more transient and problematic than social scientists once imagined; that the society contains
economic, political, sexual, and racial sources of challenge and conflict
some of which are long-standing but the seriousness of which social
science has denied and some of which in their newness expose the basis
whereon the society has been organized; that the quest for community—so earnestly pursued by individuals, so dear a goal of many
public policies, and the serious object of a growing "togetherness industry"—is more elusive than ever; and that just as individuals increasingly have come to feel powerless and rootless in their own society, this country qua country also seems to have become alienated
from other countries.

This may seem like a litany of horrors written by a pessimist on
one of his more gloomy days. All I can say is that I am reporting what
social scientists have said privately to me about their disciplines, their
society, and the rest of the world. They feel bewildered, impotent, and
unimportant in the scheme of things. And that is their question: what
is the scheme of things? Where did we go wrong? Social scientists are
like physicians who feel they have to appear to have answers, whereas
in private they bemoan how little they know and can help in most in-
stances.

Strangely, the reaction of social scientists to their bankruptcy, both
in ideas and action, shows little of the tendency to look inward, i.e., to
examine the nature of the "compliance factor" that permitted social
science to misjudge the society and events in it, to overevaluate the
contributions social science could make, and blithely to assume that
socialization into a society presents no special problems in understanding that society. Bankruptcy does not mean one is without assets but
rather that one does not have enough assets to continue to do what one
has been doing. It is the last point that I feel is so crucial to com-

prehending why when social science sought and was encouraged to participate in the formulation and implementation of public policy

> a good deal of so-called social science was proved empty or irrelevant despite the public pretense to the contrary of some academic intellectuals. It became evident that more reliable knowledge—slim though it was—frequently lay in the experiences of social workers, businessmen, architects, city managers, and politicians than in whole volumes of the social science journals. Several generations of social thought based upon determinism had produced very little of value to society. (Nisbet, 1971b, p. xviii)

In the chapters that follow I shall pursue further the major factors that contributed to social science's debacle in the post–World War II era. But this I shall do not by examining each of the social sciences but by concentrating on one of them: psychology. Aside from the fact that it is the social science I know best, there is the consideration that the post–World War II era has been justifiably labeled the age of psychology. Few fields grew so fast and became as institutionally and societally influential. And I daresay that in terms of optimism about the future and security about possessing or gaining the means to control and predict the course of events (in individuals, groups, or sectors), only economics succeeded in overevaluating itself more.

The debacle will look different in the various social sciences, but I believe that its major sources, as exemplified in psychology, are shared. The two major sources of the debacle in psychology are, first, that psychology has based itself almost exclusively on a psychology of the individual organism, and, second, that psychologists, by no means a random collection of people, never have been able to confront directly that the *substance* of their theories cannot be independent of who and where psychologists are in the society into which they have been socialized. Obviously there is nothing inherently wrong or limiting in studying individuals, and it is equally obvious that solid knowledge about individual development and behavior has been gained over the decades through psychological research. What has escaped notice, however, is that the theories generated by these studies have been, for all practical purposes, asocial. That is to say, it is as though society does not exist for the psychologist. Society is a vague, amorphous background that can be disregarded in one's efforts to fathom the laws of behavior.

This view of the individual corresponds exactly to the way the psychologist views himself and his theories; that is, the substance of psychologists' theories come from individual psychologists and are independent of the society into which they have been socialized. The theories are "objective" formulations the substance of which are independent of time, place, society, and the psychologist's place in that society. There is a dichotomy between the individual and society, between psychologist and society, and between psychologist and his theory. That these dichotomies are arbitrary, that they are conveniences that can be justified only within certain limits, that in the real world whatever it is we mean by society impacts on the individual from the moment of birth onward, that this is no less true for the psychologist than for the individuals he studies—these have not been seen as issues. You cannot see society in the same way you see concrete, palpable individuals, and as long as psychologists focus on the individual they are prevented from even entertaining the possibility that they, their theories, and the individuals they study are products of a particular society. Psychologists are aware, of course, that the abstraction "society" refers to the fact that the relationships among individuals, groups, and classes are not random affairs but rather are ordered and regulated by custom, ritual, tradition, and social history, as well as by features of the political, economic, and judicial systems. Psychologists are also aware that there are different ways that society can be conceptualized and these different ways are based on very different conceptions of what people are and can be. Yet psychologists have been content to let other disciplines deal with these issues while they pursue the fundamentals of human behavior. They are unaware that they can avoid dealing with these issues only at the expense of becoming unwitting victims of them. And that is what happened: psychologists have accepted the fiction that their theories of behavior, the pictures they contained about what people are and can be, are independent of the society into which their authors have been socialized and of their particular niche in that society.

The social sciences have long been aware that they face serious, bedeviling problems when they seek to understand people in societies other than their own. They recognize that by virtue of membership in their society their understanding of people in other societies will inevitably suffer from incompleteness and distortion. Their task is to be objective and in practice that means that one should be aware of the problem and strenuously seek to avoid its adverse consequences. This is a frail reed with which to attack the problem because it reflects a gross underestimation, indeed a gross avoidance, of the major issue: how have I been socialized to view myself, others, and my society? If the problem is one that can never be completely solved, it nevertheless must be tackled.

It is to Freud's enduring credit that he insisted that if you want to comprehend (among other things) the role of the unconscious in human development and psychological organization, you have to experience a procedure (and a relationship) that sensitizes you to the role of the unconscious in your life. To what extent the procedure meets these objectives is not an issue. The important point is that Freud recognized that the very nature of the phenomenon in others requires first that you experience it in yourself. Freud was stating a problem identical in principle to that which is crucial to social scientists: how can I understand how society is assimilated by others if I do not understand how I assimilated my society?

As I have indicated, I believe that the dissatisfaction of psychologists with psychology (a form of alienation so well defined by Nisbet earlier in this chapter) is becoming more widespread, albeit not easier for psychologists to verbalize publicly. Because this belief is crucial to my argument, I shall discuss it in more detail in the next chapter.

CHAPTER II

PSYCHOLOGISTS' DISSATISFACTION WITH PSYCHOLOGY

WEBSTER'S *New Collegiate Dictionary* (1980) gives the following definitions of crisis:

> 1a: the turning point for better or worse in an acute disease or fever b: a paroxysmal attack of pain, distress, or disordered function c: an emotionally significant event or radical change of status in a person's life 2: the decisive moment (as in a literary plot) 3a: an unstable or crucial time or state of affairs whose outcome will make a decisive difference for better or worse b: the period of strain following the culmination of a period of business prosperity when forced liquidation occurs.

Although at different times I shall use each of these definitions, in the main I shall be using the last one (3a, b), which, in contrast to the others, refers not to individuals but to collectivities. So, when I talk about the crisis in American psychology I refer to a state of affairs about which many psychologists are perplexed, compelling them to seek to understand how an era of prosperity and optimism led to the current malaise and a dysphoric sense of the future. The crisis is experienced by individuals but their understanding is that it involves far more than their personalities or life histories. It is a personal crisis in the sense that the Great Depression or World War II produced personal crises, but the person is in no doubt that he or she did not produce the crisis.

18

Crisis, like beauty, is in the eye of the beholder. In the case of American psychology the sense of crisis is by no means confined to psychologists. Many nonpsychologists (ranging from senators to so-called hard scientists, to humanists, to broadly educated lay people) look at psychology as having got its comeuppance. To psychologists they may appear to be uninformed, prejudiced people unwittingly exposing their ignorance by arrogantly making silly statements. The fact is, however, that each of the statements they have made has also been made by some psychologists. Like everybody else, what psychologists say in print or in public forums is not identical to what they say in private or informal conversation.

The Great Depression produced personal crises but certainly not for everyone. Similarly, not all psychologists experience or sense a personal crisis in relation to their field. And, again as in the Great Depression, the experience of crisis varies in substance and strength with age. But what makes the analysis of the crisis so problematic is the difficulty psychologists (like most other people) have in conceptualizing the relative contributions of personal factors and the social-structural-institutional characteristics of the field. As human beings we have the capacity to be self-conscious and to judge ourselves in a truly personal stream of time: past, present, and future. And that capacity for self-consciousness provides us with a ready-made basis for thinking about and responding to other people. We may be aware that we are different from other people but we unreflectively assume that each of these other people has the same capacity for self-consciousness that we do. We spend almost all of our lives aware of ourselves and others as discrete human beings. We can *see* ourselves (literally and figuratively) and we literally *see* others. But we cannot *see* the structure of the milieu in which we see ourselves and others. We know (part of us, and then only occasionally) that we exist in a milieu that we influence and that in turn influences us, but precisely because we cannot see that milieu the way we see ourselves and others, our explanations of our behavior and that of others tend to be narrowly personal or psychological. So, when a person senses or experiences a crisis it is understandable, albeit wrong or misleading, that he or she would resort to explanations that are narrowly psychological. It is, perhaps, more correct to say that our prepotent tendency is to overlook or vastly underestimate the characteristics of the milieu as well as of the society in which it is embedded.

There is an irony here that speaks to the personal crises of psychologists. In a most general way one can define psychology as the effort to understand the nature of the transactions between people and their social and physical surround. Implicit in that effort are three assumptions: people as bounded organisms have a comprehensible structure and organization; the milieus in which people exist have a comprehensible structure and organization; overt and covert behaviors are always a transaction between the two types of structures. Man is *in* nature, and that should render suspect explanations that focus primarily on man. The irony is in the fact that when psychologists explain their behavior as psychologists their explanations tend to be amazingly psychological. Man, so to speak, is figure and the surround is ground. Frequently, as I shall show in later chapters, it is as though the surround did not exist.

On what basis do I justify the assertion that in their roles many psychologists experience a crisis? After all, there are thousands of psychologists who have formal credentials entitling them to be called psychologists, and they vary in terms of age, site of work, specialty, and income. And there are thousands more in the process of trying to obtain formal credentials. I make no claim that I have systematically sampled from this population and determined the nature and extent to which psychologists sense a personal crisis. The justification for the assertion has several aspects, some of which will not sit right with those who rivet their attention on people as individuals. Let me start with another assertion: in the post–World War II era there has been an exponential increase in the frequency with which words like isolation, anomie, alienation, and loneliness are used in writing and speech. For anyone who reads novels (or, for example, the plays of Beckett, Albee, Genet, Pinter, and Ionesco) it is hard to avoid the impression that the modal person in our society is constantly dealing with feelings of unconnectedness and unrelatedness. If one restricts oneself to the promotional rhetoric of the group dynamics and psychotherapy movements, or to the substance of their journals, the same picture emerges: we are strangers to ourselves and others. What is different here is not the message and research findings of these different literatures but the constant barrage from all directions. Decades and even centuries before World War II there were social philosophers, sociologists, and clerics who predicted that the social forces let loose in the world would lead to what so many people today say they are experiencing.

Even if one discounts the significance of this barrage by a sizable fraction, one must, as I do, assume that we are not dealing with a transient social phenomenon. And one would not be flying in the face of contrary compelling evidence if one assumed that this sense of personal crisis is becoming more widespread. But what is the relevance of this to the sense of crisis that I conclude many psychologists experience *in their roles as psychologists?* One way of answering this question is by rhetorically asking another one: on what basis can one assume that the factors and conditions that contribute to the sense of personal crisis in people at large are not operative for psychologists? Why should they be exempt? Psychologists live in the same society and they, like others, will be affected by its features that produce the sense of crisis in or beyond work roles. What I am saying here is that if you have concluded that many people in our society experience a sense of personal crisis, you do not have to know anything about psychology and psychologists to assume that they, too, are having similar experiences.

But I do know something about psychology and psychologists. I have been in psychology for four decades, during which time I have come to know many psychologists differing in age, background, specialty, religion, ethnicity, and competence. And, of course, I know something about myself as a psychologist. Especially during the past decade I have been preoccupied with trying to understand how I came to think the way I do, why I see things differently today than before, and why in earlier days I simply missed seeing what I now think are the important problems. Put in another way, why do I feel so much less related to psychology today than ten years ago? Why did a simmering sense of crisis as a psychologist reach a hard boil and propel me to try to think in new ways (for me)? This is not the place for autobiography, but what is relevant for the present discussion are several issues that illuminate some sources of the psychologist's crisis. I call them issues but that does not mean they were clearly formulated by me. I "sensed" them as issues but I never felt willing or able to pursue or conceptualize them. I knew something was wrong about psychology and my uses and teaching of it, but neither internal nor external forces required me to deal directly with the problem. That, I know now, was not happenstance or my personality dynamics but rather a direct reflection of the conceptual crisis in psychology. I simply did not have a way of thinking that would help me understand me, my milieu, and the larger society. I was too riveted on me and other me's.

From my earliest days in college I was addicted to psychoanalysis and socialism. During the day I read Freud and at night I did my politics. I majored in psychology but learned relatively little about psychoanalysis and even less about society. I had no doubt that I had hold of two versions of universal truth and I could see no conceptual conflict between them (at the same time that I would have been very hard put to interrelate them). Socialist theory explained my external world and psychoanalysis my internal one. By the time I finished graduate school I had begun to have doubts about socialism but none about psychoanalysis. The disenchantment with socialism had two major sources: socialization into graduate school and World War II. On the one hand, graduate school immersed me in a psychology of the individual, while, on the other hand, conceptions about how and why society (even my small social world) was structured as it was became ever more fuzzy. I had become a psychologist and that meant I was interested in people, and operationally that meant studying and working with individuals.

My first professional job was in a new, large, innovative state training school for mentally retarded people. Now, almost forty years later, I can see why that institution set the stage for my doubts about psychology, the beginning of a sense of crisis as a psychologist. To put it succinctly, I came there completely unprepared to comprehend that setting—for example, its organizational structure; the history and traditions of that structure; the dynamics of the relationships among the setting, the judiciary, the state legislature, and the executive; and the selective factors determining who came to work in the school. In all my years there I saw, thought about, and dealt with people and only in the vaguest way was I aware that my behavior and that of others could not be explained by my knowledge of psychology. Whatever conflicts I experienced—and the base rate of conflict in that type of setting is not low—I explained in terms of my own and others' personality and cognitive characteristics. And if someone had asked what were the significances of this setting for understanding American society, I blush when I think how I would have answered the question. I probably would have said it was an interesting question and then gone on to say that it said something very positive about our society, (and there were not many positive things I was in the habit of saying about our society).

One could argue that I was young and naive in those days, which, of course, is quite true. And one could say that I had had a very parochial education and that I should not confuse *my* narrow education with that of other psychologists. I accept this argument if it means that had I gone to graduate school elsewhere I would have gained a deeper and broader grasp of psychology. But the argument is invalid if it means that I would have obtained a better preparation for understanding milieus, culture, social history, and what for brevity I shall call the social fabric. It is probably true that if I had gone to what in those years were considered the best graduate departments of psychology, I would have been more securely imprisoned in a superrigorous individual psychology.

In 1949, three years after I left the Southbury Training School, I wrote *Psychological Problems in Mental Deficiency* (1959). The word "psychological" in the title is quite appropriate because that book deals almost exclusively with the "minds" of individuals. Words like culture, institutions, society, and history appear frequently in the book but their conceptual content is virtually nil. This may have been the first book in the field to discuss issues surrounding the applicability of psychotherapy to mentally retarded people, and I probably was more proud of that chapter than of any other because I thought I was shedding light on the workings of the minds of people for whom psychotherapy was supposed to be inappropriate. To understand why I judge the book so differently today, and what contributed to a somewhat clearer sense of crisis as a psychologist, I have to talk about Dr. Thomas Gladwin. Tom was finishing course work for his doctorate at Yale in anthropology preparatory to going to Micronesia to do a "culture and personality" study, which was the rage in those days. He took a course with me in projective techniques because he planned to use them for studying individuals on the island of Truk. When he asked me whether I would be willing to interpret the protocols he would obtain, I readily assented, largely because I believed that through these techniques I could ferret out the intricacies of the human mind wherever one encountered it. I had done a fair amount of reading in anthropology, found it fascinating, but the fascination had far more to do with my curiosity about the seemingly endless variety of people on this earth than with what this diversity meant for psychology as a discipline. It was like psychoanalysis and socialism: interesting but unrelated conceptually in my mind. After five years on Truk Tom returned, and for one year we worked extremely closely, becoming lifelong friends.

The point here is that for the first time I was close to someone who saw and understood people in a way different from mine. Tom saw individuals *in* society. He could reverse figure (the individual) and ground (society) with facility and come up with relationships or questions that altered subsequent perceptions of figure and ground. I would accuse him of not understanding people and he would accuse me of not understanding the nature and force of culture and tradition. We were both right, but in the quest of the right I knew that Tom was "righter." I had to conclude that there was much in my way of thinking and acting as a psychologist that screened out issues and possibilities that, if I recognized them, would be more than I could or would want to handle. I was too much the psychologist.

The effects of my continuing relationship with Tom can best be seen in a monograph we did for the National Association for Retarded Children (Sarason, 1959; Sarason and Gladwin, 1958).* This monograph is discernibly less psychological than the first edition of *Psychological Problems in Mental Deficiency*. An even clearer indication of how my thinking changed is the fourth edition of the book, co-authored with John Doris, a psychologist who is really a scholar of social history. John is another example of a highly trained psychologist who over his lifetime has been breaking out of the confines of his discipline. But John had the advantage over me in that he had by virtue of ethnic and religious background (and God knows what else) acquired a Jesuitical appreciation of knowledge, past and present. And if the curious reader will compare our last book (1979), *Educational Handicap, Public Policy, and Social History: A Broadened Perspective on Mental Retardation,* with the early editions of my first book, he or she will see how much my thinking has changed. But what the reader will not discern are the tensions and crises that accompanied those changes. The fact is that I no longer regard myself as a psychologist. This is not said with disparagement of psychology as a discipline because that would be a kind of argumentum ad hominem. It would also be to indulge psychologizing: trivializing a complex problem by resort to a motivational psychology of the individual, precisely what I have been arguing against.

*In chapter 7 I discuss Gladwin's (1980) *Slaves of the White Myth: The Psychology of Neocolonialism,* a book notable for the ways in which Gladwin describes his crisis with anthropology, a direct consequence of reexamination of his society and how it had socialized him and his field.

I have been autobiographical not to convey any sense of superiority, or to parade the steps I have taken on the unmarked road to wisdom, or because I now have a vision of the truth. The phenomenological facts are otherwise, and writing this book is testimony to a continuing struggle and sense of intellectual crisis. Indeed, the only reason I have been autobiographical is to assure the reader that I have an acute sense of crisis in regard both to psychology as a discipline and to how I use *any* psychology as I do. So, it will bother me not at all if the reader thinks I am a nut, or a woolyheaded character, or an undisciplined, misguided imcompetent asking unclear or unanswerable questions. What I ask of the reader is that he or she believe that I have had and continue to have a sense of crisis—something has been wrong, is still wrong, but what road should one take? However, my sense of crisis is obviously no basis for concluding that other psychologists are having a similar experience. What has permitted me to talk about my sense of crisis is that in discussion with me numerous other psychologists unambiguously have articulated a similar experience. All have expressed feelings of dissatisfaction with and unrelatedness to psychology as a discipline. Before saying more about what these psychologists have said to me I must explain why I trust their reports—and when I say ''trust'' I refer to the feelings expressed and not to the rationale for them.

Several years ago I got interested in how highly educated professional people experience their work, an interest that had some personal relevance. By the time I became interested in the problem my thinking about psychology and our society had reached the point where I felt secure in assuming that what I experienced in my work was not (could not be) peculiar to me. Having made that assumption, I was forced to make another assumption: it is extremely difficult for highly educated professionals to talk candidly about how they experience their work. As I noted in the preface, we define ourselves, and others define us, largely in terms of our work, and perceived dissatisfaction with our work can be very upsetting and have adverse consequences in all areas of our living. Some people do not like to think about it except now and then, for others it is a chronically gnawing irritant associated with feelings of impotence or being ''locked in''; and for others a kind of live volcano that literally forces them drastically to alter the shape and direction of their lives. It took me years to recognize this obvious point: when a person makes a lifelong commitment to a line of work, and when society says that that work is important, fascinating, and fulfilling, it will not be easy for that person to face the possibility that a wrong choice has been made. As I wrote in *Work, Aging, and Social Change: Professionals and the One Life–One Career Imperative* (1977), our society has made it more difficult to change careers than to change marriage partners, although the dynamics are identical. And parts of that difficulty are the internal and external barriers to confronting the consequences of dissatisfaction in work.

It is not fortuitous that mainstream psychology (however defined) has never been interested in the experience and structure of work in our society. Allied fields have a huge literature on work but precious little of it is about highly educated people like psychologists and other social scientists. To be interested in such groups requires that you accept at least three assumptions: the experience and nature of work have to be seen in terms of the society's ideology, the economic basis of and among the sites and organizations where people work, and the variety of functions that work serves; when large segments of the population find their work uninteresting or feel unrelated to the products of their work (they *labor,* they do not *work*), one has to examine the role of changes in the social-economic-ideological fabric; and when the relationship to work has become problematic for increasing numbers of lesser educated people, it is very likely that the social changes bringing this about are having similar effects on more highly educated people. The experience of work is far less an individual matter than we like to think. How people come to their work, how they select it and are selected by others, and how they and others come to place different values on different kinds of work are functions of the social order and its underlying justifications. Where people are in that social order mightily determines how they define themselves in relation to work. As suggested earlier, one would never know from the psychological literature that where psychologists are in the social order is not the result of random social processes. Instead, one gets the picture of psychologists disembodied from the social order; that is, their work, theories, and practices are seen as functions of individual factors and circumscribed milieus, not of features of the social order.

Put in another way, psychologists, like most other people, do not see themselves *in* society but rather see themselves *and* society, a dichotomy that has made it easy for them to avoid confronting directly the nature of that society. To accept the assumption that how one experiences work (its substance, uses, and changes) is in large part a function of where one is in the social order would require psychologists to see communality between them and other groups that the socialization and education of psychologists make it easy to ignore. They unwittingly accept the myth that they can understand themselves and their field in relatively asocial terms. Satisfaction or dissatisfaction in their work is seen as a psychological, not a social order, phenomenon. The way in which psychologists view psychology and the social order will occupy later chapters. Here I wish only to indicate that changes in, and explanations of, the ways psychologists experience their work and field, as well as the candor with which those changes can be articulated, are fundamental theoretical issues (if only because they concern how and why psychologists think as they do) not even hinted at in psychological theories, each of which centers on the individual organism and virtually dismisses the social order.

When I decided to find out how highly educated professionals experience their work, I started by reviewing my own personal dynamics and by making lists of all the people I knew, or had known, or with whom I had had some meaningful contact in the previous five years. They were very long lists (inevitably incomplete) and the persistence necessary to get up these lists was frequently beyond me. I felt absurd doing it. How do you play back and make sense of five years? What kept me going was the insight that from the standpoint of how these people experienced their work (needless to say, many of them were psychologists) I had been listening to but not hearing them, just as I had been listening to but not hearing myself. What impressed me was the number of people who had expressed to me a clear sense of dissatisfaction with psychology as a science or profession. One could argue, of course, that I was *now* hearing what I wanted to hear. To this legitimate possibility I can only report the spontaneous responses I got from psychologists who read the book on work (Sarason, 1977). That book was only minimally concerned with psychologists but its central themes, I assumed, were no less relevant to them than to those we interviewed: largely people in medicine and law. And what these psychologists, in person or in writing, expressed was a distinct sense of crisis as psychologists. Some found their work as psychologists no longer interesting; others said they felt little or no relationship to psychology as a discipline; a few viewed their years of professional preparation to have been largely wasteful; and a majority said they no longer were able to read psychology journals or most books about psychology. One chairman of a large department of psychology wrote to say that although what I had written was not true for him, he thought it applicable to a sizable minority of psychologists. I regarded these responses as evidence for the conclusion that the sense of crisis as a psychologist was not peculiar to me; they did nothing to disconfirm the validity of my feeling that it is inordinately difficult for any professional to come to grips with dissatisfaction with choice of work.

There are many reasons a psychologist may be unhappy in his or her work. A psychologist may be unhappy with the work setting (e.g., type and size of organization, hierarchical structure, and colleagues). He or she may be dissatisfied because income is not enough (and may never be enough) to permit a desired lifestyle. A psychologist may be unhappy because he or she is not getting recognition for work well done. And, of course, family and marital struggles can rob a psychologist of much of the satisfaction derivable from work. And in these days of economic retrenchment one's vision about work and status can become cloudy and unpleasant.

When I talk about a sense of crisis as a psychologist I am not referring to any of these possibilities. I am referring to something that is more narrowly conceptual, although it may become related to these other sources of dissatisfaction. Specifically, by the sense of crisis I refer to the following: one regards psychological theory as arid, or outmoded, or grossly unrelated to the real world, or so circumscribed as to be trivial; one regards reports of psychological research (certainly the great bulk of it) as incomprehensible, or pointless, or ludicrously rigorous, or lacking any semblance of rigor, or simply boring; one regards psychological practices and techniques (e.g., clinical, educational, industrial) as pseudoscientific in their grounding, or far from effective, or used in questionable ways for questionable purposes; and in whatever strengths and combinations these views are held they are accompanied by feelings of anxious drift, unease about the future, and dysphoric musings about "how did all this come about; where did we (I) go wrong?" To put it metaphorically, the love affair with psychology seems headed for termination because the object of love is no longer attractive. What explains the overevaluation of that love object? Why does it seem so different now? Should I abandon it? How? With what consequences? What will take its place? I do not wish to convey the impression that a lot of psychologists are obsessed with this sense of crisis and that in their professional work they are coming apart at the seams. I do maintain that many psychologists are at least fleetingly aware of this sense of crisis, and for some it is more than fleeting. I also believe that this sense of crisis has become more widespread in the past two decades, affecting different age groups in psychology in similar ways. To understand this development requires discussion of some of the features of post–World War II history, especially in regard to the meteoric growth, in numbers and influence, of the social sciences.

With the close of World War II three attitudes gained ascendancy; a new world had to be built and the less resemblance to the pre–World War II era the better; natural science could give us heretofore undreamed of possibilities for bettering material welfare (as well as for destroying society), and we had to develop the knowledge and means to insure that these possibilities would be used to promote human welfare; and it was a responsibility of government to stimulate and underwrite the growth and quality of higher education so that the highly educated scientists and professionals who would be needed to build a better world would be available. (Government responsibility for elementary and secondary education came somewhat later.) The emphasis on higher education was based not only on a moral responsibility to help millions of veterans rechart their lives or to provide them with personal and medical services but also on the view that a transformed world would require a quantity and quality of natural and social scientists then in short supply.

It is unfortunately the case, as Nisbet (1973) and others have shown, that the dynamics of war stimulate in a society bold, creative thinking that leads to new knowledge and techniques that produce lasting changes in that society. World War II may well be the clearest example. There is hardly a major idea, theory, or technical innovation in contemporary life that cannot be shown to be a rather direct descendant of developments during World War II (see Garner, 1972). World War II impressed officialdom with what natural and social scientists could do and, no less significant, impressed the scientists with what they did and potentially could do once the war was over. This was certainly the case with psychology, which before World War II was a small, academic, laboratory and experimentally oriented discipline having relatively few meaningful ties with the world of affairs.

As World War II approached, and then began, psychologists

flocked or were drawn into the war effort either full-time or as consultants. It was a new world for them, faced as they frequently were either with problems that were unfamiliar or with problems for which existing knowledge was inadequate (or misleading). Vision, audition, neuropsychology, attitude formation, propaganda techniques and analysis, personnel selection, psychological casualties and treatment, educational handicaps among recruits, and counterintelligence—dealing with these areas had several major effects on psychologists and, therefore, on psychology. First, psychologists felt needed in ways and to a degree they had not experienced before. Second, they could not avoid the conclusion that prewar psychology had been conceptually parochial and whatever its merits had been they were not adequate to the problems of the real world. It was not that they felt psychology should become more applied or practical but rather that its basic theorizing and conduct of research would have to be altered. Third, their war experience convinced psychologists that they had much to contribute on both a policy and a research level to coping with the staggering transformations (social and scientific) they envisioned in the postwar era. Fourth, certain influential psychologists felt that psychology had a moral obligation to direct some of its efforts to training people who would be doing applied work, e.g., clinical psychologists who would be employed in the many scores of clinics and hospitals the government would build to serve veterans. Here, too, the goal was to provide practitioners with a solid grounding in psychological theory and research without which the quality of their services would be impoverished. They would be psychologists first and clinicians second; they would use their clinical work not only to help people but also to further psychology as a science. Fifth, plunged as many were during the war into positions of public importance, and fascinated as many were by being in or around arenas of significant public decisionmaking (like the swirling, dizzying, ever challenging wartime Washington scene), some psychologists were eager to maintain contact with that scene once the war would be over.

The growth of psychology after the war, in terms of numbers and diversity, was phenomenal. No less significant than that growth—and for my argument more significant—was, as I emphasized in the previous chapter, the optimism of psychology about what it would achieve as a science and what is could contribute to the betterment of man. It was onward and upward. It was not only psychologists who proclaimed that we had entered the age of psychology (Sarason, 1975, 1977); people generally became enamored of understanding the human mind. Psychoanalysis became academically respectable and therapeutically the "best" form of treatment; Skinner's (1972) *Walden Two* became a best-seller; Spock's (1945) advice to parents about how to rear children was heavily psychological and, in light of the quantity of books sold, seemed to reassure millions of parents insecure about how children should develop; and the number of young people seeking to become psychologists and psychiatrists seemed infinite. The demand for psychologists far outstripped supply.

Psychology after the war was not alone in its optimism—a general phenomenon at least in the natural and social sciences. If you were an ordinary citizen who listened to the radio (later TV) and read newspapers and mass circulation magazines, you might have had difficulty feeling optimistic; indeed, you might have concluded that the world was going to hell rather quickly. It seemed as though daily there was an international incident that would bring about another world war. Greece was in turmoil, Lebanon was no better, the Berlin blockade made everybody jittery, China had its revolution, and then came Korea. If these were all manifestations of a cold war, what would a hot war look like? And, of course, there was the testing of atom bombs in the Pacific, convincing many people the world would soon end not with a whimper but with an atomic bang. Within our own boundaries the picture was not a peaceful one either: titanic struggles between labor and industry, the emergence of the "urban problem" into public awareness, escalation of black consciousness and militancy, the formation of a militant civil rights movement (well before the sixties), the 1954 desegregation decision soon followed by the frightening confrontations in Little Rock and some Louisiana parishes, and the ominous shenanigans of Senator Joseph McCarthy. And when President Truman fired General MacArthur, a popular hero, more than a few people lived through those weeks with a fear of Bonapartism.

It is hard to review the history of the fifteen years after World War II with satisfaction. And yet, during those years academia had a basically optimistic stance in several respects: universities were expanding as though expansion would go on forever; federal policy was based on the assumption that research was a necessity if societal problems were to be better understood and dealt with (a policy with which the universities of course agreed); and faculty members found themselves shuttling between campus and Washington at the behest of officials seeking their advice. Yes, there were serious problems in the world but if society really backed social science the way it had been and was backing natural science, the impact of these problems could be blunted. The economists were optimistic that they had the knowledge and tools to fine tune the economy. Sociologists were in an era of grand theorizing that, they thought, would make society more comprehensible and manageable. Political scientists (together with economists) created the field of policy science and, as the name suggests, believed that this new approach would avoid the mistakes of the past. Anthropologists, very few in number before the war, became valued resources as the country assumed worldwide responsibilities; they were no longer viewed (or viewed themselves) only as experts in regard to so-called primitive societies but also as people who had something to say about understanding and changing our society. And then there were the psychologists, who envisioned all kinds of breakthroughs in applying newly acquired knowledge of the human mind to the betterment of private and social man. I am not aware of any studies on the matter but it is my impression that in both university and government psychologists assumed positions of influence disproportionate to their numbers at the time. The fifteen years after World War II saw the meteoric rise of the National Institute of Mental Health, which funded training and research in many fields of psychology. Psychology promised a lot, much was expected from it, and the money and facilities to realize its promise were made available. Remember that at this time the mental health fields, into which psychology had willingly entered, had convinced themselves and others that they had (or were about to have) the psychological equivalent of aspirin: a scientifically based, research evaluated, effective psychotherapy.

What gave psychology such optimism? I have already suggested that a large part of the answer was the zeitgeist of the natural and social sciences, a consequence of World War II. But this answer obscures something that is relevant to the sense of crisis that many psychologists later experienced. The fact is that there were psychologists who were against psychology's involvement in the world of affairs. That such opposition would exist and that it would be reflected in a major institutional form like departments of psychology in universities were not predictable from psychological theory. That is to say, psychology provided psychologists little in the way of concepts that would help them understand what was happening in an institutional sense. Those in opposition had no way of understanding what was happening except in terms of an individual psychology and, strangely enough, the same was true for those moving out of the more familiar confines of psychology. That is why name calling was so easy, i.e., differences were "explained" by personality variables, with which psychology had an abundance. It was the good guys vs. the bad guys, the type of thinking that makes Westerns interesting movie fare and very lousy social analysis. I tried elsewhere to describe this trend. It is in a paper "Psychology to the Finland Station in the Heavenly City of the Eighteenth Century Philosophers" (Sarason, 1975):

> I would like to suggest that for psychology the doors to the heavenly city were flung wide open with the onset of World War II. Almost overnight, psychology was given the opportunity as science and practice to demonstrate how it would combat evil and human misery. Elsewhere I have described in some detail what happened. Suffice it here to say that "basic" and "applied" psychologists—in the heavenly city some people are more equal than others because some possess more of the truth than others—directed their efforts to saving and protecting our society. And, again almost overnight, with the war's end psychology began to grow in terms of numbers, specialties, scope, and ambitions. And who doubted that this was other than progress? If before World War II the American Psychological Association had a couple of thousand members, and two decades after the war it had over 30,000 members, were not those hard data testifying to progress? And if you wanted basalt-like hard data, there were the dizzingly astronomical expenditures by government for scientific undergraduate majors and production of PhDs (the doctorate testifying to a successful communion), and, finally, the increase in journals. How much more evidence was required to prove that everyday in every way we were learning more and helping more?
>
> There were, of course, G. Stanley Hall's latter day saints who worried about and fought against the inclusion of the applied psychologist in the church of science. These saints were not opposed to growth and progress but rather to the possibility that these softheaded people—whose methods were impure, whose dedication to "true" science was suspect, who too easily confused facts and beliefs, and who sought equality without earning it—would vulgarize the true science. As one of them (Samuel Fernberger) said about these strangers, they would "cook the goose that laid the golden eggs." Contained in the metaphor is a view of the past history of scientific psychology—a string of golden eggs—en-

dangered by the present interrupting the march of progress. Like the
Hebrew religion which eschews proselytizing because of its special truth
and mission, the "true" scientists wanted little or no commerce with
strangers. Stay pure, keep to the fundamentals of objective method, mine
and mind the gold, and posterity will bless us for our courage and devotion, because we will have given to posterity the true answers to man's
nature and problems. We are and shall be faithful to the commandments
of science because they point us to salvation. Thou shalt worship no other
God but science. Monotheism was not threatened.

The purists were a minority. Here and there they were able to keep
their enclaves pure, but overall the integration between the hard- and
soft-headed came about, not by a supreme court decision but by the
pressure of external society and fatefully, federal money. Psychology as a
science and practice were married. Let us bypass the possibility that there
are grounds for annulment because they never really slept together.
(Each member of the marriage has accused the other of impotence,
deceit, and other of man's less endearing attributes, sexual or otherwise.)
As a collectivity, however, psychology presented itself as miner of scientific gold and as distributor of it to a waiting society. There was hardly a
sphere of societal functioning in which psychologists did not become a
notable part: business, industry, schools, hospitals, government, the
military. Even religious establishments wanted scientifically to select personnel and were receptive to the use of psychotherapy, founded, of
course, on basic theory and "good" research. When I look back at the
past three decades I am impressed, not very positively, with the vast array
of solutions psychologists came up with to the problems of individuals,
groups, institutions, and the larger society. Just as the basic, hardheaded,
scientific psychologists had no doubt that they were doing what was in the
best interest of society. Despite what the purists feared, the softheads
(at least on the level of public utterance) prided themselves on their scientific training and ability to use reason. (Did they not have doctorates
which testified to their training in scientific methodology?) There was
more than envy in the quip by clinical psychologists that a psychiatrist
was a psychotherapist with a PhD. And let us not forget that during this
period a lot of hardheads ventured out of their laboratories as consultants
to diverse settings with problems. At the level of practice, you could not
tell the hard- from the softheads without a scorecard.

For all practical purposes—and I mean practical—neither the
purists nor the softheads had ways of understanding how the transformations of psychology in an institutional-structural sense were highly
correlated with transformations in other parts of society and that both

transformations were correlated consequences of societal transformations (national and international) engendered by World War II. These conflicts within psychology signaled the emergence of three clusters of psychologists. The first were those who did not relish seeing psychology move in new directions, and a number of these psychologists increasingly felt unrelated to the field. A second cluster, tending to be younger in age, were those eager to relate psychology to the study of pressing social problems. And then there was the third cluster: a growing mass of young people seeking to enter psychology precisely because it held such promise for changing the world. One could say there was a generational and political struggle going on in psychology between "conservatives" and "radicals," between "pessimists" and "optimists," between the "hardheads" and "softheads." Government policy and funding for training and research in psychology were decisive in resolving the political struggle.

Paradoxically (but only on the surface), from the vantage point of the eighties many psychologists in the second and third clusters have come to feel like those in the first cluster: uncomfortable in relation to their field. It is my argument that the three clusters were in similar ways conceptually unprepared to deal with the world as they defined it. Not only was the first cluster intent on unraveling the mysteries of the individual human psyche; it did not see as relevant to its purpose unraveling the intricacies of the social structure in which individuals are born and develop. The structure of the mind was figure, all else was noise, and flexibly reversing figure and ground was rare. Take, for example, three of the most influential pre–World War II books: Allport's (1937) *Personality,* Murray's (1938) *Explorations in Personality,* and *Frustration and Aggression* by Dollard and co-workers (1939). These splendid contributions were deservedly influential but they showed the defects of their virtues: the individual is always center stage and society is background. And if one compares the depths to which these psychologists plumbed the structures of the individual mind with those to which writers of social psychology texts went in their analyses of society, the former really come up smelling roses. The fact is that when psychology steered itself postwar toward the arena of everyday social problems, it had no way of realizing that it was basing its efforts on conceptual grounds identical to those of psychologists in the first cluster. What really would be surprising is if it had been otherwise, because those who were doing the steering had been trained by those who were fearful of contaminating psychology with the germs of the social world. Overcoming the substance and consequences of one's socialization into a field is not simply a matter of an individual's psychology; a lot outside the individual has to happen for us to overcome our socialization, and what we overcome is always partial at best.

I started this chapter by discussing my belief that in recent years a growing number of psychologists have begun to feel disaffected from psychology. I then went on to suggest that this disaffection stood in marked contrast to the optimism that radiated throughout psychology during its rapid growth in the fifteen years following the war. That optimism, however understandable and refreshing as a social phenomenon, had a conceptual basis that was woefully inadequate for dealing with social, political, and cultural phenomena and processes. What happened in the sixties to change optimism to pessimism, to produce the present crisis in which psychologists seek to understand what went wrong? A great deal happened, far more than I can even allude to here. But one generalization can be made: every psychologist began to think about, and somewhat fewer began to be involved in action in regard to, the turmoils of that decade. The involvement may have been formal or informal, spontaneous or coerced, but in one way or another, many psychologists qua psychologists became activists seeking to change, influence, or moderate behavior, policy, and events.

The reader would be quite wrong if he or she inferred that those who became involved represented a limited segment of psychology. Those were really the days when you could not tell the purists from the softheads without an academic score card. Civil rights, gay rights, women's liberation, the war on poverty, black militancy, Head Start, urban social explosions, Vietnam, Students for a Democratic Society, the Weathermen—those were not restful days and psychologists (among others) got caught up in the social hurricane. They tried or were asked to be "relevant," and that word, overworked as it was, accurately reflected what many psychologists wanted to be. Psychology, they said, as a science and a profession should not be aloof from the social process.

Elsewhere I have characterized the stance of many psychologists during this period in the following way (1975):

There was a brief period, from the end of the 1960s to the very early

1970s, when the hard- and softheads had the equivalent of Pope John's Vatican Council. For that brief period they seemed in agreement that neither of them had had a correct view of the heavenly city. Mea culpas were heard around the land.

We have worshipped false Gods! Far from creating a just society, we had contributed to the level of injustice! Far from loving our fellow man we, as individuals and collectivities, had unwittingly reinforced man's inhumanity to man (which includes men's inhumanity to women)! We must exorcise arrogance, social insensitivity, and moral obtuseness from within our personal and scientific selves, as well as from the educational and governmental institutions of which we were part or for which we share responsibility! It was not quite Mao's cultural revolution during which the universities shut down for two years, but it leaned in that direction, and there were some whose moral fervor caused them to regret that it did not fall that way.

But why did so many hardheads and softheads feel that they had been misled themselves? The answer is not a simple one, but neither is it terribly complex. Most simply put, the answer that was given was:

We had put our faith in a concept of science that said science would provide us with those kinds of truths which would set us free to build the heavenly city. Formulate the problem clearly, study it rigorously and impersonally, find out where your thinking went wrong, reformulate the problem, make your findings public, listen to the criticisms of others, and so on, until the compelling power of the truth overcomes all resistance in others to its recognition and acceptance. The scientific truths and their applications to people and society is the realm of values: the shoulds and the oughts. Science and technology did not build and drop the bomb in Hiroshima. That statement omits the fact that *many people first had to say it would be the right thing to do.* Science and technology did not put man into outer space; *people first had to say it was the right thing to do.* When we praise or blame science for its social consequences we are praising or blaming our values, our judgments, the bases upon which we choose to act. When the discoveries of genetics present us with mind-boggling possibilities for selective breeding, science cannot tell us how to choose. Between discovery and action are the questions of how shall we live together and by what values. The question is not only what genes we want to pass on but what values we want to pass on. If science can afford to be neutral, we cannot. Living is too important to be left to the scientists and their hard or soft findings.

Whatever guilt, individual or collective, psychologists may have felt about past insensitivities seemed not to alter their conviction that psychology had a great deal to contribute to the general welfare. Guilt and optimism are not antithetical. So what happened to psychologists on the way to the public forum? Let us listen to an eminent economist whose book *The Moon and the Ghetto* (Nelson, 1977) should be required reading for every social scientist:

> The search for "the Great Society" entailed highly publicized efforts at turning the policy steering wheel. Broad new mandates were articulated—the war on poverty—and specific policies were designed to deal with various aspects of the problem. The histories of these departures clearly identify the key roles often played by research reports, social science theory, formal analytical procedures. More recent years have seen an increasing flow of proposals for organizational reform: vouchers for schools, health maintenance organizations, greater independence for the post office, a national corporation to run the passenger railroads, pollution fees, revenue sharing. It is easy to trace the intellectual roots of many of these ideas. The technoscience orientation has come later, and never has had the thrust of the others. Nonetheless the intellectual rhetoric has been strong, and has generated at least token efforts to launch the aerospace companies on problems of garbage collection, education and crime control, and programs with evocative titles like "Research Applied to National Needs."
>
> The last several years have seen a sharp decline in faith, within the scientific community as well as outside, regarding our ability to solve our problems through scientific and rational means. Those who want to get on with solving the problems obviously are upset about the loss of momentum. It is apparent that many of the more optimistic believers in the power of rational analysis overestimated that power. There are strong interests blocking certain kinds of changes. Certain problems are innately intractable or at least very hard. But the proposition here is that a good portion of the reason why rational analysis of social problems hasn't gotten us very far lies in the nature of the analyses that have been done. John Maynard Keynes expressed the faith, and the arrogance, of the social scientist when he said, "The ideas of economists and political philosophers, both when they are right and when they are wrong, are more powerful than is commonly understood . . . I am sure that the power of vested interests is vastly exaggerated compared with the gradual encroachment of ideas." But, surely Abe Lincoln was right when he made his remark about not being able to fool all of the people all of the time. . . .

In addition to their clumsy treatment of value and knowledge (a problem that seems to infect analysts generally), analysts within each of the traditions have had a tendency to combine tunnel vision with intellectual imperialism. . . . Members of the different traditions have had a tendency to be lulled by their imperialistic rhetoric. This has often led them to provide interpretations and prescriptions that the public, and the political apparatus, rightly have scoffed at. Failure to recognize the limitations of one's own perspective has made analysis of problems that require an integration of various perspectives very difficult. Indeed a kind of internecine warfare obtains among the traditions over the turf that lies between them. (Pp. 16–17)

Most psychologists who entered the arena of social action left it disillusioned. They came with data and solutions, but even when they had neither they assumed that their training and capacity for rational thinking, their ability to pose clear problems and find appropriate methods leading to solutions, would establish their credibility as well as their right to an important role in rational social change. Most of them did not realize, if only for their lack of knowledge or respect for social history, that they were fully agreeing with Karl Marx, who had said it is not enough to try to understand the world—you have to try to change it! But when they tried to change their world, even a small part of it, they experienced massive frustration. Some came to see that world as ungrateful, others thought it impossible, and many came to view it as incomprehensible. Somehow that world did not bend to the ideas and purposes of the psychologist.

There were psychologists, of course, who early on learned, as did psychologists who left the academy to play a role in the World War II period, that the nature and scope of psychology ill prepared them for what they wanted or were asked to do. Some of these psychologists concluded that the core problem stemmed from naivete about how to apply psychological theory and data to the real world. That is to say, there was nothing radically wrong with psychological theory and data but there was a lot wrong with the way we went about applying them. As a consequence, a vast literature appeared on institutional and social change. Phenomenologically, one might put their stance this way: we were not prepared to be good social engineers and our job now is to figure out how to become better engineers; the bridges we started to build were obviously going to fall down, and our task is to build bridges that will stand up. This stance left psychological theory relatively intact; that was not where the problem was. There were psychologists who thought that psychological theory was grossly inadequate or irrelevant, but they were unclear about why this was so and could offer no substitute formulations. They did not blame the outside world for psychology's failure. Paradoxically, these psychologists were of two very different types. The first were psychologists who had long been skeptical about what psychology was and where it was going, and for them the travails of psychologists who had entered the public forum were empirical confirmation of this belief. These psychologists were not opposed to those who ventured forth but they saw little connection between psychology as a body of theory and knowledge and the behavior and thought processes of psychologists in action. The second kind were primarily in the so-called hard parts of psychology; they had great respect for psychological theory and knowledge but felt that it was an injustice to this new science to embroil it in the seamy world of social action. They tended to view activist psychologists in terms of "with friends like these you do not need enemies." The best thing that psychology could do for society would be to continue to till the fertile soil of the scientific endeavor. If these two kinds of psychologists were not bedfellows, if they took very different views of the status of psychological theory and knowledge, they at least agreed that society, in its efforts to change itself, would be better off if they did not take psychology seriously.

The undercurrent of malaise in psychology is general to the social sciences and the society at large. Where did things go wrong? Why do we feel unable to exercise control over our fates? Why did well-motivated and well-funded efforts fail or fall so short of the mark? Are we really banging our heads against a wall of intractable problems? Why are we so gun-shy about making, or becoming involved in, new efforts? Why is it so difficult for us to generate optimism about the significance of our individual efforts or government action? These are questions that people are asking themselves.*

The crisis in psychology is a real one albeit relatively unverbalized because it is so difficult for psychologists to confront directly the conse-

---

*A good example of the change that has taken place centers around the term "change agent." In the sixties there was a steady increase in the number of people, many in psychology, who labeled themselves change agents. It was a badge of honor and courage. In the seventies one hardly heard people calling themselves change agents. Today, the label has a quixotic ring to it.

quences of the possibility that the conceptual underpinnings their field provides them for the daily roles are, at best, inadequate and, at worst, an obstacle to be overcome.* From what I have said in this chapter one might conclude that the crisis is more widespread and poignant among psychologists in those parts of the field that focus on the social or cultural or institutional or developmental features of human behavior. Although I think that is the case—and my conclusion about a crisis is based largely on discussion with such psychologists—I shall endeavor in later chapters to suggest that the conceptual shortcomings that helped produce the crisis pervade the entire field. The fact is that all of American psychology (with some notable exceptions) has been quintessentially a psychology of individuals. When early in this century Thorndike put one rat in the maze (and not two or three or more), he was reflecting and reinforcing a focus that continues to dominate psychology. If one wants to understand why the thousands of research studies on human learning have done little or nothing to improve our schools, one has to recognize that generations of educational personnel were reared on a psychology of individual learning. So, although the crisis is experienced more in some than in other parts of psychology, its roots touch all parts.

Let me state what I have *not* been saying. I do not claim that American psychology has not produced useful theories, data, and applications. Nor do I claim that the sense of crisis psychologists are experiencing is a *direct* consequence of American psychology's conceptual limitations—as if such a crisis with its personal and professional ramifications for different kinds of psychologists were explainable simply by "bad theory" or some other form of psychologizing. And,

---

*More than anyone else Gergen (1973, 1976, 1978, 1979a, b) has pinpointed the narrowness of psychology's theories and the discipline's failure or inability to probe the roots from which these theories sprung historically, i.e., to state and take distance from the picture of man that psychology is painting. Gergen makes it clear that it is a fiction to think of psychology and its theories as substantively independent of time, place, social history, and world views, which are imprisoning to the extent that they go unexamined. Unlike most psychologists, who see only the living present (including the world of ideas and theories) as essentially discontinuous with the past, Gergen shows how much of that past still governs the substance of the field, steers it down blink alleys, and is at the center of its conceptual malaise. There are many points of overlap between the thrust of Gergen's writings and what I have to say in this book. I place greater weight on the consequences for psychology of its emphasis on the individual and the almost complete failure of psychology to see itself as a product of a particular kind of society.

finally, I do not believe that the crisis is of such proportions, in terms of pervasiveness, strength, and clarity, as to lead one to expect that great changes are in the offing. What is in the offing is the possibility that the tensions within and the dissatisfactions with the formal institutions of psychology (e.g., the American Psychological Association) will no longer be contained or sealed over by rhetoric and reorganization. The American Psychological Association is not a tower of Babel but it is well on the way to becoming one (some psychologists would consider this judgment to be excessively charitable). What is significant is that the crises of individual psychologists exist side by side with institutional tensions. This is not happenstance, although the interrelationships have hardly been articulated.

In this chapter I have made several claims. First, many psychologists feel disaffected from their field. Second, this disaffection has many sources and one of the major ones is what I have, in summary fashion, called the dependence on a psychology of individuals. Third, this dependence has not been without its merits, but the failure of psychology in the past two decades to live up to its self-proclaimed promise requires that we reexamine what we heretofore took for granted or, more correctly, never bothered to think about. When crises of individual psychologists exist at the same time that the institutions of psychology are in turmoil, and the society at large seems bewildered and drifting from upheaval to upheaval, the reexamination that needs to take place cannot be modest in its purposes.

The purpose of this chapter has been to explain why I think psychologists are experiencing a crisis in relation to their field. In later pages I shall begin to illustrate more concretely and in some detail what I mean by the conceptual crisis in American psychology, the nature of which has contributed to psychologists' sense of disaffection. But before we get to the conceptual crisis we must deal with a part of us that is unconceptual, is in all aspects of our being, and is hardly sensed, let alone articulated, by us. I refer to the fact that each of us has a world view, a weltanschauung, that we have not acquired in any conscious way, that is never taught explicitly, but without which what we say, think, and believe would make no sense. Psychology has never warmed to the significance of the weltanschauung, in part because of its embeddedness in European philosophy and in part (like Freud's unconscious) because it has seemed to lack the characteristics of a scientifically testable concept. As I shall endeavor to show in the next chapter, each of us has a world view that compasslike directs us even though we are unaware that we are not doing the steering. That world view is both cause and effect of a social order, and it is for that reason that to probe psychology's relation to the social order requires that we examine the concept of world view.

CHAPTER III

THE SIGNIFICANCE OF
A WORLD VIEW

THERE ARE DIFFERENT PERSPECTIVES from which eras are seen and labeled but one thing all such perspectives have in common is that they try to make sense of a past. The label may purport to describe the present but if that label catches the public's favor (or specialized segments of it) it is because the label suggests a relationship between past and present. The relationships the label is intended to suggest may be either continuous or discontinuous in nature, although the latter is far more frequent than the former: the sizzling sixties versus the silent fifties, the conforming seventies versus the sizzling sixties, the Dark Ages versus the Middle Ages, and so on. The further we get in time from the labeled eras the more reluctant we are to emphasize sharp discontinuities and the more impressed we are with the slowness with which an altered way of thinking becomes pervasive. Strangely (perhaps not?) this reluctance seems in no way to inhibit the tendency to interpret our own era as one of quick change. Indeed, there is now a sizable literature that tells us that the distinctive feature of our era is the speed with which changes in society and world views occur. Our problem, we are told, is how quickly to unlearn customary ways of thinking in order to adapt better to the fast pace of change. It is hard to avoid gaining the impression that we are at best in a "two steps forward, three steps backward" situation; that is, our ways of thinking simply cannot keep up with the pace of change. There is no doubt that this

44

message fits the phenomenology of many people, and if there are
dissenters it is because they feel that "two steps forward, three steps
backward" is a gross indulgence of optimism bordering on delusion.
But the message is descriptive and prescriptive rather than ex-
planatory, more in the nature of the "how to do it," narrow engineering tradition. Implicit in the message is "if you can't lick 'em, join
'em": we are in an era of quick change and, like it or not, we had better adapt to it.

There is another literature, far more serious and historical, that attempts to understand the origins and long-term development of our
customary ways of thinking, how they affected and were affected by
the shape of social institutions, and the conditions that contributed to
disjunction and conflict between custom and action. Contemporary
problems were not born yesterday and they will not go away tomor-
row. According to this view, the past is still in the present and our task
is to confront and understand that the problem is not somewhere out
there but inside us. The reason we see and experience so much turmoil, the reason we are so dissatisfied with the ways our society has
dealt with its problems, and the reason we should not look with
unrealistic optimism toward the future is that we are, and will continue to be for some time to come, prisoners of a world view into which
we were too effectively socialized.

There is still another perspective from which the contemporary
world appears to be in such a state of moral, political, economic,
religious, and philosophical flux that it is impossible and even fool-
hardy to try to discern the shape of things to come. An old world is dy-
ing and a new one is being born. Depending on temperament and alle-
giances (and a good deal more) you may greet the passing of the old
world with hosannas or with the pain of nostalgia. In my experience,
most people, regardless of age, sex, race, and religion, have given up
trying to understand the world as it is and cannot generate enthusiasm
about the future. The one thing they feel secure about is that quick
and drastic change is the hallmark of our times.

Someone once said that it is hard to be completely wrong.
Whatever truth such a statement has is applicable to these different
perspectives. The thrust of this book is consistent with the view that
one of the sources of our difficulty is our inability to fathom our world
view. It is more correct to say that the difficulty originates in the lack
of recognition of the fact that every person has a world view. The dic-

tionary definition of weltanschauung is "a comprehensive conception
or apprehension of the world, especially from a specific viewpoint."
Most people would not see themselves as having a comprehensive conception or apprehension of the world, let alone a specific viewpoint on
which such a conception is based. To some people the word "world"
refers to the earth, sun, planets, and all that is beyond them, and they
would maintain that they have not the faintest idea how to conceptualize the world, i.e., to say on what basis it is organized. They can
see part of this world and may accept the facts that there are worlds
beyond, that there are people who have ways of studying and understanding these beyonds, and that these same people somehow got a
man on the moon and brought him back. These people, they would
say, have a comprehension of "the world" but they themselves have
no such conception. What these people are confusing is knowledge
with weltanschauung. They are unaware that they are telling us that
they have a weltanschauung: there is a universe, it is presumably
lawful, there is no point in their trying to understand it, they are in
that universe but not in a way that has practical meaning for their
daily lives, they take on faith that this universe is and increasingly will
be knowable, it really is a mystery bordering on the miraculous, and
they are less than pygmies in this universal scheme. But they also are
telling us that this world view has a special viewpoint: their ignorance.
And in telling us about this world view, they also indicate that people
are divided into at least two types: those who understand, or seriously
try to understand, the universe and those who do not or cannot. If we
were to pursue systematically the world view of people, we would find
that it is comprehensive and has a special viewpoint. One's view of the
universe is interwoven with one's view of people. However one con-
ceives of the universe, it is connected to how one sees oneself in relation to other people, the social world. A weltanschauung is literally
about the whole world—things and people.

One does not choose to have a weltanschauung. It emerges and
develops over a lifetime. It may change in certain respects but rarely in
regard to its origins and bases, which remain silent and axiomatic.
One's weltanschauung is more than knowledge and less than language. What one calls knowledge is largely a consequence of weltanschauung and not its cause. The knowledge one receives from others,
and the way one receives and organizes such knowledge, reflects a
view of man and the world. The infant and young child are unaware of

this process but those responsible for rearing the child are quite aware that they are inculcating a way of viewing self and world. But they, like the child, are unaware of how much of what they are trying to do bears the imprint of a particular weltanschauung. Why they had the child, how the child should be cared for, how the child should respond, what it should learn, how it should talk, how it should dress, how and about what it should think, what it should become, what its rights and needs are, what it should be protected against and prepared for—about these and many more questions parents can give answers without the slightest recognition that these answers derive from an unarticulated world view having a special viewpoint. The answers may be justified by knowledge or experience, and they always contain the shoulds and oughts about living, but their derivation from unverbalized axioms about the nature of man and the world (physical and social) is neither sensed nor examined.

We are inevitably prisoners of time, place, and culture. The significance of history lies far less in the facts unearthed or the events described than in the determination of the weltanschauung, about which people are largely unaware but without which the facts and events cannot be comprehended. A weltanschauung is not motivated; it is received, imbibed, a kind of given, a basic outline within which motivation gets direction. Unlike Freud's unconscious, always striving for expression, the world view is always expressed in our language, ideas, goals, actions, and perceptions. Take, for example, the well-known graphic representation of a New Yorker's conception of the rest of the country and world. It is humorous but, like so much humor, Steinberg's cartoon startles us into recognizing that each of us literally has a picture of the world. The picture may vary depending on whether one is a New Yorker, a Londoner, or a Muscovite but each of us has a picture from a special viewpoint. We are not accustomed to thinking about the picture, let alone drawing it, but there *is* a picture that says a good deal about how we see ourselves (and, therefore, others) in relation to our spatial world. That picture is given to us, so to speak, as much as we create it. And those pictures are never neutral in connotation. When in the past people (e.g., Copernicus, Galileo, Newton) presented a picture that conflicted with or contradicted the traditional view of the world, heated controversies erupted and lives were threatened because the new picture called into question a weltanschauung about man, the universe, and God. To accept the new picture required a new world view and that was *unthinkable*. It was unthinkable in two ways: it was unthinkable within the context of the old picture, i.e., it could not be derived from it; and once the new picture presented its challenge, people did not know how to think about it except by rejecting it.

A weltanschauung orders life: its past, present, and future. It is only when events external to us pierce and crumble our world view that we see how much of that view we had unreflectively accepted as truth about ourselves and the world. Blacks being taken into slavery, Jews walking to the Nazi gas chambers, immigrants forced to go to new lands, American Indians uncomprehendingly facing white settlers, countless colleagues of Stalin's sitting numbly and dumbly in prison cells—these people understood by its shattering that they had had a world view, one they could no longer rely on. More than that, their world view had been so much a part of them that they could never take distance from it. (In roughly the same way we approach definitions in a dictionary: we accept them; why on earth should we challenge them?)

At some point in each of my seminars I say to my students (I do not ask): "I bet you believe in progress." The first response, and it is an immediate one, shows itself in a somewhat startled, quizzical facial expression. I can always count on at least one student's breaking the silence by asking what I mean.

> I bet you believe that the world is better off today than it was one hundred or five hundred years ago, and that one hundred years from today the world will be better off than it is now, assuming there is not atomic catastrophe. You not only believe that we know more than people in the distant past, that we can do more and control more, but also that people today are far wiser and more free. That is to say, the human race has been on an onwards and upwards course and it will go on that way.

The students become uneasy because saying what I do in a challenging manner suggests that I disagree with what I think they believe. And I do win the bet. They believe in progress. More important, they rarely have questioned this aspect of their world view. It would be wrong to say that they take progress for granted because that implies they have ruminated about the issue and made a conscious choice to believe in progress. On the contrary, in their world view alternatives to a belief in progress are unthinkable. They do have a picture (literally a picture) of man today and in the past that leaves no doubt about who is better off morally, physically, politically, and intellectually. And they can adduce all kinds of facts that justify their belief in human progress. When I tell them that there are societies in the present, as there have been in the past and probably will be in the future, that do not subscribe to this view of human progress, either they are unimpressed or they explicitly put down these other societies. When I present them with what seems to be an endless list of the human slaughters that have occurred in this century—and I never have a problem giving them an account of the latest one from the front page of the daily newspaper—they are bothered but the aspect of their world view pertaining to progress remains unchanged.

The intent of my challenge to the students is to get them to begin to see that they have a weltanschauung, which by virtue of the effectiveness of its acquisition requires no examination and yet gives meaning and direction to experience. For most people world view and weltanschauung are intimidating terms associated with erudite minds (e.g., Hegel, Kant, Herder, Marx, Vico) with a proclivity for obscure writing. Less erudite people, regardless of their place and status in society, would rather believe they possess no world view or possess one that is so undifferentiated as not to be dignified by scrutiny or a pretentious sounding label. Aside from being intimidating, the term "world view" escapes clear definition: it is not an attitude in the conventional sense, nor is it formally acquired and organized knowledge or an articulated value or set of values; in part it is visual-perceptual, a way of imagining and ordering space and relationships among natural phenomena, near and far, terrestrial and beyond, heaven and hell (for some people). It is a picture incomprehensible without the artist, and yet it is in no conscious sense created by the artist. Indeed, the person is ordinarily unaware that he has such a picture, and when he does so realize, he experiences little or no organization among its parts. He is at the center of his universe, although he does not see himself that way. This aspect of the world view may change as a result of unusual perceptions associated, e.g., with a first airplane flight, a first trip across the ocean, watching the first man on the moon, seeing or experiencing a natural catastrophe, or observing an unidentified flying object. The change may be temporarily great but more often than not the effect of a single experience is small.

The weltanschauung is a kind of map, as much for traversing and understanding the world as for representing what it looks like. Another feature of the picture is that it is far more oriented to present and future than to past. But that is illusory because, as we shall see later, the weltanschauung has an axiomatic past, so axiomatic that its existence in and significance for the picture of the present and future go relatively unnoticed. An example of this is the response of people to Darwin's theory and description of evolution. I make the assumption that for most people at that time, in relation to their daily living, their picture of the world incorporated few signposts of the distant past: animals were animals, fish were fish, man was man—each was distinct and had a distinct place and function. That's the way the world is and that's the way it was. If they were religious, they could "explain" the shape of that world, a world that was not their construction. Who constructed that world was, of course, important to them but largely in terms of a picture of a future evolving from a present. Darwin's writings literally presented a very different picture of the world. The violently adverse reaction to Darwin is usually described in terms of challenges to beliefs, theories, and attitudes and that, of course, is true. But it is equally true that the response to the challenge stemmed from instant recognition that one had a picture of the world that someone else was calling erroneous. It was in principle not unlike the response of people to the early outcroppings of modern art: they could not "see" the picture or accept it as a way of representing some aspect of the world. These paintings were not their visual-perceptual representations of reality and they were proof of the artist's craziness, i.e., crazy people *see* the world in crazy ways. This rejecting response established the fact that people had a picture of the world at the same time that it signified how unexamined that picture would remain.

Today we are all familiar with the concept of body image; that is, we have a picture of what we look like, what we looked like, and what we will look like. But when we say we "have" the picture we do not mean what we mean when we say that we have fingers. We do not see the picture of ourselves with anything like the clarity with which we see our fingers. That picture is not "there" the way fingers are. Indeed, most of the time we are not even aware that we have a picture of ourselves unless some unusual circumstance forces us to describe that picture. And when we are forced to do so, we then realize that we do have what appears to be a fleeting, fragmented picture that involves all parts of our body, our style of movement, dress, and appearance. We experience (when forced to) the picture as fleeting and fragmented (like some modern art) but if we persist in the task of representing that picture we begin to see that it does have some organizing principle or principles. It is a picture that is part of a larger one of our world. And just as our body image is mightily revealing of us as persons, so is our picture of the universe. But it is a picture we rarely look at or try to comprehend. We have the picture but we are unaware of its significance in our scheme of things. It remains isolated from and unconnected with our ideas, theories, and actions. It is not disconnected because that implies that there was once a connection: it is and has been unconnected. As we shall see later, this unconnectedness has mischievous consequences for how we deal with and try to change our world or that of others.

How do people react when they are told that they now live in one world? In a cognitive sense they know that what happens in one part of the world can affect other parts. Behind the one world message is another one: we have to learn to understand and live with diverse societies. It is the second message that is in sharp opposition to the picture people have of their world. When you examine the imagery in people's minds when they think of other societies and the people in them, the label "one world" is the last one that would seem appropriate. It is a picture highly differentiated in terms of geography, architecture, spatial relationships, qualities of people, and modes of transportation and action. This picture is experienced as real, a faithful replica of the way things are, and we are unaware that it is the result of socialization. The more educated and sophisticated we are, the more we think that our world picture stems exclusively from study, knowledge, and conscious experience. This myth founders on a number of facts but chief among them is that many of these people acknowledge, publicly or privately, that their world picture simply has not had the consequences in action they expected. It would be more correct to say that they are puzzled and disappointed about the course of events but that their world picture has changed little. There is such an identity between one's picture of self and one's picture of the world that drastically upsetting experiences alone can change these pictures.

The existence and significance of world pictures have long been part of the stock-in-trade of anthropologists. Indeed, it has been the anthropologist who has emphasized that the world picture is an integral aspect of the weltanschauung. Part of the fascination of anthropological reports is the fact that there are people whose visual-perceptual picture of the world is utterly different from our own. But what is our own? Can we explicate ours the way the anthropologist has for those in the cultures he or she describes? You can recognize that there are different world pictures but that in no way means that you have and can describe your world picture. You may even think you understand why other people have a world picture different from your own without understanding (or seeking to understand) why you have the one you do. And if you pursue the shape and dimensions of your world picture, you confront the most thorny issue of all: what limits to understanding does one world picture set for another?

Anthropologists are very much aware of this issue and try to cope with it. As Gould (1969) notes in the epilogue to his fascinating book *Yiwara: Foragers of the Australian Desert:*

> Our sojourn at the Warburton Ranges and in the Gibson Desert in 1966–67 placed us amid a state of flux. I was able almost simultaneously to satisfy my curiosity about the nature of a traditional hunting and foraging way of life in the desert and to observe the essential changes being brought about by white contact. To be sure, my evaluation of the traditional nomadic life of the Aborigines is subjective in the sense that it is based on close personal experiences rather than on data which can be tested and measured objectively. Other fully competent scientists may disagree with my estimate of Aboriginal life, but I did not have any built-in sympathies for the Aborigines before we arrived in the desert. My appreciation of them arose from my experiences with them, not from any romantic ideal or image of the "noble savage"—an attitude which, indeed, anthropologists nowadays are rigorously trained to avoid. (P. 191)

If Gould did not have a romantic picture of the noble savage, that does not mean he did not have a picture. When he read about these Australian aborigines, and when he decided to go to study them, we can assume that he had all kinds of pictures of what the people looked like, how they appeared in action, how they might greet him, and how the forbidding geography would appear. We can believe Gould when he says that he tried to avoid distorting preconceptions derived from his very different physical and social world. But just as you cannot stop the tides, you cannot stop your imagination or tell your world picture to take a vacation. When Gould says that he did not have any built-in sympathy for the aborigines, he is telling us a good deal about part of the picture of himself as well as about that of anthropologists in general. It is a picture in which one sees oneself as dispassionate and objective until, as in Gould's case, one deliberately engages in close personal relationships with those one is studying. Before he went he was "objective"; once he got there he was "subjective." Other anthropologists, he says, could remain far more objective than he did. Gould is telling us that in his picture of people, in this case anthropologists, their appearane as well as their actions may tell us nothing about their insides because they want to experience the outside uncontaminated by what is inside them. Gould seems defensive that he does not fit that picture, which requires us to note that in the picture there are data and people who are doing things with them. Unfortunately, Gould never directly tells us about his world picture before and during his study, although he leaves us in no doubt that his world picture changed.

However, there is one part of Gould's pre-Australia world picture that can be described and it is one that is central to the thrust of this book. What images or pictures or visual fantasies were conjured up in his mind when he thought about himself in regard to the aborigines he was going to study? He was thousands of miles away from them but the picture unfolding in his mind placed him on their site and in their midst, watching, talking to, and interacting with them. To Gould, as well as to most of us, there is nothing questionable about that picture. We understand the picture (its substance as well as process) and why Gould has it. On what basis can one question it? One could ask what permits Gould to develop a picture as preparation for action in regard to the aborigines. What permits Gould to accept the picture and the actions they will give rise to as right, natural, and proper? His world picture is explicit about his *right* to pursue a course of action. It is a picture in which the relations between people (Gould and the aborigines, we and they) are unreflectively structured to permit a person in one culture to study people in another. Now let us hear what Gould has to say following the passage quoted above:

> In looking back I also realized that my experience involved a sharp irony which is true, in varying degrees, of the field experiences of other an-

thropologists. The technology and specialization which have enabled Western society to invade remote parts of the world and change the lives of the native inhabitants have also produced anthropologists and enabled them to learn about these peoples and their traditions. As long as the Gibson Desert Aborigines remained isolated, they remained unknown. When their isolation was broken and they became known, they began to change with phenomenal speed.

At the Warburton Ranges Mission, right before our eyes, my wife and I had seen the transformation caused by closer contact with whites, as desert families settled there. From tiny beginnings their dissatisfaction with their lot has grown rapidly to Western proportions, accelerated, no doubt, by the recent boom in mining. The Aborigines who had lived there longer were even more blatant in expressing their dissatisfactions. The rise of petty thievery at Warburton and the recent looting by Negroes and others in American cities, though a hemisphere apart, are both manifestations of the same deep discontent and dissatisfaction which are essentially characteristic of Western civilization. (Pp. 191–192)

Gould's world picture has changed dramatically. It depicts him, the aborigines, and anthropologists in general in ways his prestudy picture never hinted at. There is a strong note of regret—at least some serious soul searching—that he and other anthropologists had a world picture that contributed to what he now considers undesirable consequences. More than that, the world picture these paragraphs suggest not only takes more of the world (past, present and future) into account but also reflects a different relationship among people.

The extent to which a person's world picture changes and the extent to which the person is aware that a previous picture was incomplete or faulty are consequences not of ideas or beliefs but of compelling perceptual experience. When Gould says, "at the Warburton Ranges Mission, right before our eyes," he is being literal, not metaphorical. When what one sees cannot be fitted into one's world picture, changes in aspects of that picture become possible. (The more common case, I suspect, is that the world picture is so unreflectively assimilated that it prevents reinterpretation of perceptual experience.) Other aspects may remain unchanged. Take, for example, the picture Gould paints for us about petty thievery and looting as "manifestations of the same deep discontent and dissatisfaction which are essentially characteristic of Western civilization." What picture gets conjured up in the mind about Western civilization? It is a picture with two major parts:

Western civilization and all other civilizations. Neither part is further differentiated in time and space. In one part people are depicted in antisocial actions presumably absent or much less frequent in the other part. It is hard to avoid the conclusion that one part is populated by ignoble savages while the other part contains noble savages, the image that Gould and other anthropologists are studiously taught to avoid. People in one part would look unhappy and discontented, while people in the other part would look happy and satisfied. It may not be a picture of the differences between heaven and hell, but it tends in that direction.

Alterations in significant aspects of a world picture always involve a sense of loss, which becomes represented in the picture. Gould is helpful again, and poetically, in this regard:

> While I do not advocate the Australian Aborigines or other people like them into perpetual "zoos" or preserves away from white influences, I must admit to feeling that mankind as a whole may be suffering an irretrievable loss with the passing of their societies. We will never again know firsthand how it felt to lead the sort of foraging and hunting life that man has lived throughout most of his past.
>
> Today the Gibson Desert is the loneliest place on earth, lonelier even than the wastes of Antarctica. What can be lonelier than a place where people have lived their lives and then left forever? Now the same sense of melancholy that blankets an ancient ruined city covers the Australian desert, where the sandhills lie silent in the blazing sun and the gleeful shouts of children chasing a lizard through the spinifex are heard no longer. (P. 192)

I have been emphasizing the world picture part of the weltanschauung for three reasons: everyone has a world picture but tends to be unaware of its outlines and contents; the world picture is a means by which we see, traverse, and interpret the world; and the world picture is a function and depiction of the power, political, social class, religious, ethnic, racial, and gender relationships in a particular society at a particular time. It is the last reason that is of major importance because it is from the world picture that one can deduce the axioms without which the picture and the other parts of the weltanschauung make no sense. By axioms I mean implicit, unverbalized (usually) statements that require neither thought nor examination. They are given to us and we take them. So, for example, the anthropologist in training does not have to be taught that he or she has a right to study and write about people in other cultures. He does not say to himself or herself "I have a right to go and live with and study this Australian aboriginal tribe." Nor does the anthropologist have to say to himself or herself "I have a right to make public through publication what I saw, experienced, and concluded about these people." Although these kinds of rights have a kinship similar to those we in this society call constitutional rights, they do not require a written form and they do not stem from a long, wellknown, and well documented history in which the constitutional convention of 1787 played a major role. If we were to challenge the anthropologist about this right, its derivation, and its justification, the first response might very well be incomprehension or disbelief. When I queried an anthropologist along these lines, he looked at me with suspicion and puzzlement and after a while asked: "Do you mean how do I justify morally what you call rights or actions?" I told him that I was not (yet) interested in morality but rather in where these rights come from and why they have been so unreflectively assimilated by him. Obviously, I said, people in other cultures do not possess these rights and probably every person in every culture studied by an anthropologist has given up trying to comprehend what the anthropologist was about. To which the anthropologist replied by describing the uses of science, the disinterested search for knowledge about man and the world, and the benefits that accrue for improving man's welfare, self-knowledge, and control over an impersonal, dangerous, and capricious physical world. But, I had to reply, you have introduced a moral note because you justify the rights by their good consequences, and in doing so you mean good for the people who possess these rights. You do not have to be much of a historian to conclude that a lot of people never have experienced the desirable consequences.

We shall return to these issues in chapter 7, where I discuss a book by the anthropologist Thoman Gladwin in which he describes a transformation in his weltanschauung so drastic that he no longer considers himself an anthropologist. Let me now turn to a series of brief assertions for which the previous pages have been prologue and with which the rest of this book will be concerned. For the sake of clarity and simplicity these assertions will be about the social sciences, especially psychology, although I believe them to hold for every human endeavor regardless of the categories into which people place themselves or others put them.

1. Every psychologist has a weltanschauung the substance and pictorial aspects of which are parts of his or her definition of the nature of people and the world. This weltanschauung is largely implicit but pervasive in its effects on thinking and action. One cannot choose to have a weltanschauung; one has it. It is the silent background that gives shape and meaning to the figural aspects of experience.

2. Although we know about the crucial significances of the weltanschauung in societies different from ours, past and present, that knowledge is itself in part shaped by and assimilated into our weltanschauung. Such knowledge is rarely a spur to explication of our weltanschauung.

3. Within a particular society a person's weltanschauung is generated and developed by many factors; chief among them are those associated with social place and status. Every society has a social structure and where one is in that structure is fateful for the weltanschauung. It would be wrong to say that these factors cause a weltanschauung because a weltanschauung can be as much a cause of place in the social structure as it can be an effect. However, despite these differences in weltanschauung, people in the same society will, to varying degrees, share aspects of the same weltanschauung.

4. Psychologists, like other social scientists, see themselves in the tradition of science. Specifically this means they have an interest in and questions about man and the world that, in order to be satisfied, require formal, communicable theories on the basis of which a variety of actions can be taken to prove or disprove hypotheses derived from the theories. These theories and research actions, in marked contrast to the weltanschauung, are explicit and supposed to be uncontaminated by any personal characteristic of the theorist. The theory is separated from the theorist; it becomes objectified, has thinglike characteristics, and can be used by others. The theory, like the weltanschauung, paints a picture of man and the world, but, unlike the weltanschauung, it is highly and rationally organized, containing no or few unknowns. With rare exceptions, it is a picture deliberately restricted in scope. As substance and process, weltanschauung and formal theory are poles apart, but they coexist.

5. As a science, psychology has long justified itself on the basis of its contributions to knowledge. From its formal beginnings a hundred years ago, and for decades after that, psychology was unconcerned with the applications of its scientific findings. It professed an interest in promoting human welfare but that was a far-off goal and not the responsibility of the pure scientist. What this view implied about psychology and psychologists—who they were, where they came from, their place and status in society, the social organization of that society—was never scrutinized. In short, there was no inclination to examine this position in its relationship to an implicit picture of man, society, and the world. This did not change when changes in the world (e.g., the

world wars) plunged psychology into social action. Psychology was not pushed into social action, it willingly and eagerly became related to and embedded in society in new ways. These events certainly affected the world view of psychologists but they had little or no impact on the form, substance, and direction of psychological theory and research, except to give them more status, resources, and social influence. Psychology was enabled to do more of what it did in the ways it did them. This implied a weltanschauung having several axioms: man and the world are knowable *and* controllable; what the good society should look like is clear; the knowledge that psychology has and will obtain about man is independent of time, place, and the scientific psychologist; psychologists understand how the society is organized; as a scientific endeavor psychology can have no adverse consequences for psychologists and others in the society. There is another feature of the psychologist's world view that deserves special emphasis.

6. The world views of psychologists, directly reflected in their formal theories, are about individuals (bounded and discrete) who have internal structure and substance. These individuals can appear different in myriad ways but they share psychological functions and structures. These functions and structures are both pictorialized and conceptualized.

Psychologists not only studied and theorized about these structures and functions, they *saw* them, just as pictures of the individual were conjured up in the minds of the readers of those theories. What those pictures were, why they took the form they did, and their derivation were questions that avoided scrutiny. When theorists clashed with each other, it frequently had far less to do with data than with different but unexamined pictures of what man is and should be. According to one of the axioms underlying the concentration on the individual, if you really understand the psychological structure of the individual, you have the means either for changing or for controlling or helping him (in those days there was no her, another feature of the weltanschauung). There was a related axiom: conceptually organized knowledge *should* be the primary, if not the exclusive, basis for action. Given psychology's concentration on individual structure, there was no place in the weltanschauung and formal theory for how society is structured. The individual was figure and all else was amorphous ground. Unlike the composer for whom figure (melodic line) and ground are an indissoluble unity, one not being more important than the other and each depending on the other, the psychological theorist disembodied the individual from the social context. But this was another variant of how psychology as a field was disembodied from its place in society. Psychology was "there" in the world picture, a very differentiated part of it, quite in contrast to the social context.

7. With World War II and its aftermath, psychology became embedded in more parts of the society than ever before and in ways that reinforced its weltanschauung. Psychology became tied to various public funding sources,

and this was also true for the private and nonprofit sectors. Science, and therefore psychology, became objects of public policy as much because policymakers expected great benefits from the scientific endeavor as because scientists promised these benefits. If the weltanschauung of psychology changed in the two decades after World War II, it was in the strengthening of the axiom that the social world is knowable, predictable, and controllable and in the related axiom that breakthroughs in understanding the individual human mind would be basic building blocks for a better society. Then came the tumultuous sixties. Almost overnight, psychology (and the social sciences generally) as a science and a profession was called into question by articulate groups in society as well as by some psychologists. Psychology's theories were said to be narrow, trivial, and unrealistic; its theories and practices were discriminatory; its ethical and moral base was self-serving and irresponsible; and it had misled itself and society about what the good life is and how to achieve it. For purposes of summary one could say that *largely by virtue of who psychologists were, and where they were in the social order, they had developed theories and procedures that rested on an amazingly superficial and distorted conception of the structure and history of the society and therefore they produced a very faulty picture of how individuals become what they are.* This amounts to no less than a criticism of the weltanschauung of psychologists. Needless to say, it is a criticism that brings to the fore the obvious fact that new world views had emerged in the society.

8. This criticism, and the national and international events and changes from which it derived and which are still taking place, has had pervasive effects on psychology and psychologists. Of particular relevance here is an increasing disaffection among psychologists from psychology. The disaffection, rarely voiced publicly and directly, is not of a piece but it does contain an acceptance of much of the criticism: trivialization of both trivial and important problems; arid, formal microtheories that serve to fill scientific and professional journals and secure recognition (and promotion) for their creators; failure of the promise of psychology (moreover, there appears to be no new base from which to move in new directions); puzzlement about what lessons should be learned from what has happened and even uncertainty about what has happened and why; gloom and pessimism about the future of psychology and the world; and anxiety about psychology's retrenching economic base.

In the next chapter I shall be more concrete about what I mean by psychologies of the individual and their enormously adverse consequences. Before turning to the next chapter, it will be helpful to the reader if I quote a child developmentalist (Kessen, 1979):

THE BELIEF IN THE INDIVIDUAL AND SELF-CONTAINED CHILD

Hovering over each of the traditional beliefs mentioned thus far is the most general and, in my view, the most fundamental entanglement of technical child psychology with the implicit commitments of American culture. The child—like the Pilgrim, the cowboy, and the detective on television—is invariably seen as a free-standing isolable being who moves through development as a self-contained and complete individual. Other similarly self-contained people—parents and teachers—may influence the development of children, to be sure, but the proper unit of cultural analysis and the proper unit of developmental study is the child alone. The ubiquity of such radical individualism in our lives makes the consideration of alternative images of childhood extraordinarily difficult. We have never taken fully seriously the notion that development is, in large measure, a social construction, the child a modulated and modulating component in a shifting network of influences. The seminal thinkers about children over the past century have, in fact, been almost undeviating in their postulation of the child as container of self and of psychology. Impulses are in the child; traits are in the child; thoughts are in the child; attachments are in the child. In short, almost every major theory of development accepts the premises of individualism and takes the child as the basic unit of study, with all consequences the choice has for decisions that range from selecting a method of research to selecting a therapeutic maneuver.

Uniform agreement on the isolable child as the proper measure of development led to the research paradigms that have dominated child psychology during most of its history; basically, we have observed those parts of development that the child could readily transport to our laboratories or to our testing sites. The use of isolated preparations for the study of development has, happily, been productive of remarkable advances in our knowledge of children, but with the usual cost of uniform dogma, the commitment to the isolable child has occasionally led child psychology into exaggerations and significant omissions.

There are signals now aloft that the dogma of individualism, both in its claim of lifelong stability of personality and its claim that human action can be understood without consideration of context or history, is under severe stress. The story that Vygotsky told 50 years ago, the story of the embeddedness of the developing mind in society, has finally been heard. The image of the child as an epigenetic and continuous creation of social and biological contexts is far more ambiguous and more difficult to paint than the relative simplicities of the traditional and culturally justified self-contained child; it may also illuminate our understanding of children and of our science.

The Present Moment

The cultural epigenesis that created the American child of the late 20th century continues, and so does the epigenesis that created child psychology. Necessarily, there is no end of the road, no equilibrium. Rather, the transformations of the past 100 years in both children and child psychology are a startling reminder of the eternal call on us to be scrupulous observers and imaginative researchers; they may also serve to force our self-critical recognition that we are both creators and performers in the cultural invention of the child.

Pithily and politely, Kessen has called into question the world view of psychologists, especially in relation to their focus on the individual organism. As we shall see in the next chapter, this emphasis has characterized psychological theory and research since their formal beginnings in the modern era.

CHAPTER IV

PSYCHOLOGISTS AND THE SOCIAL ORDER

AMERICAN PSYCHOLOGY'S EMPHASIS on the individual is long-standing. It is not that psychology "decided" that such an emphasis would be more profitable than other directions. For our purposes it is sufficient to say that the direction taken seemed right, natural, and proper. Besides, it seemed to allow psychology to make fruitful use of scientific methodology and, therefore, to justify its separation from philosophy. For almost a century this emphasis has been productive, permitting its severe limitations to go relatively unnoticed. Recognition of these limitations is very recent. In order to illustrate these limitations I shall look at a problem with the following characteristics: it will be familiar to all readers; it has spawned a vast research literature; it has been at the center of issues of public policy and institutional practice; and it continues to elicit controversy. The problem is the conception and measurement of human intelligence, it being obvious to all that how this problem is formulated and studied has very practical social significance.

It is not relevant to my purpose to get into the substance of the issues, e.g., competing theories, statistical methodologies, and sampling procedures. What makes this problem relevant here is that it typifies the asocial, individual emphasis of psychology. When theoreticians developed their conceptions, they always had in mind the individual psyche. When researchers sought to study and validate these conceptions, they, too, focused on individuals. And, of course, when these conceptions were deemed to have sufficient validity and practical importance to be put in the format of a psychological test, psychologists used them to make decisions fateful for the lives of individuals. As a way to begin to see this point from a different perspective let us go back to a psychologist whose work was influential in determining how generations of psychologists would conceptualize the problem.

When people hear the name of Alfred Binet, they immediately think of intelligence tests, a view that puts him in the category of the engineer, i.e., someone who "designed" a way of measuring intelligence. That view gained a lot of credence because many leading psychologists devoted their lives to improving his tests, to making the tests more reliable and valid. But Binet was far more than an engineer. Long before he started to develop intelligence tests he had done a great deal of thinking about and research on the developmental aspects of human abilities. (It says a good deal about Binet that he is one of the few psychologists to whom Piaget expressed a debt, and that had nothing to do with Binet's scales.) What most people do not know about Binet, especially in regard to his scales, is that he was a social activist. In most accounts about Binet we are told that the French government asked him to spearhead an effort to pick out those children with intellectual handicaps in the Parisian schools who were in need of special educational facilities. The fact is, as Wolf (1973) has indicated, it was Binet who organized the groups that put pressure on the government to take action about the schools. For Binet the situation in the schools was morally scandalous because children, both retarded and normal, were being shortchanged. He was a passionate advocate for the mentally retarded because he was so knowledgeable about what went on in schools. How knowledgeable he was can be seen in the following statement from Wolf:

> Along with the warnings about pitfalls in selecting special class pupils, Binet added others of a completely different nature: there were teachers, he said, who would try to get rid of annoying pupils by recommending them for these classes; others who were unconvinced that the backward students were anything other than lazy; teachers of special classes who would retain pupils now ready to return to regular classes, in order to maintain their enrollment levels; parents who wished to "protect" their children, or, on the other hand, who wanted to take advantage of getting rid of them in special residential schools, and so on. In other words, he

had found mixed motivations for the "identification" of children for special education. (P. 306)

What was unusual about Binet, a very astute clinician in thinking about and working with individuals, was that he also had an appreciation of the characteristics of the social contexts in which individuals found themselves. These contexts were of two kinds: the context in which the assessment of the individual was made and the context (e.g., the classroom) for which the individual assessment was to be a basis for remedial action. In the first context the individual was center stage for the psychologist and all else was assumed to be a constant ground. The second context was far more complicated, a fact that Binet appreciated but did not pursue in any serious or systematic way. Indeed, his "mental orthopedics" for the classroom teacher centered around what one did with the individual pupil, as if teachers in the classroom teach individual children.*

In point of fact Binet recognized a third context: the social-cultural milieu in which children develop. French society was not homogeneous and the factors that made for heterogeneity had to be taken into account if one were to understand a particular child. So, when Binet focused in his testing on the individual child, that child was figure but in the background were these other contexts. But they were, for all practical purposes, very much in the background. Binet's time and energies were devoted to the development of means for testing individual children.

Binet's thinking shows a failure to take seriously his conception that intelligence is not a "thing" but rather a label we give to certain features of the ways people have commerce with their milieu (Wolf, 1973):

> We are a bundle of tendencies; and it is the resultant of all of them that is expressed in our acts. . . . It is, then, this totality that must be evaluated. . . . The mind is one, despite the multiplicity of its faculties; it

---

*Phenomenologically, the teacher always responds to a child in terms of the group of which both are a part, and the child responds on a similar basis to the teacher. It is surprising how this obvious fact has been ignored by educational theorists, who continue to talk as though teachers teach individual children. Even teachers are frequently unaware that their response to an individual child cannot be understood without taking account of the basis for the class's structure and rationale, i.e., what I have labeled the "constitution of the classroom" (Sarason, 1971).

possesses one essential function to which all the others are subordinated. . . . Considered independently from phenomena of sensitivity, emotion, and will, the intelligence is before all a process of knowing that is directed toward the external world, that works to reconstruct in its entirety, by means of the little fragments that are given to us. . . . Since all this ends up in inventing, we call the whole work an invention, which is made after a comprehension . . . that necessitates a direction. . . . It must be judged in relation to the end pursued; therefore, we must add criticism. Comprehension, inventiveness, direction, and criticism; intelligence is contained in the four words. (P. 204)

What Binet was after was a way of ascertaining the major components of an individual's intellectual processes. *But his own conception of these processes required an analysis of the context in which the assessment would take place because if intelligence is not a thing but ways of having commerce with one's surround, what are the characteristics of that surround?* The feature of that surround to which Binet gave the most attention was test items. They were the stimulus materials and they were assumed to be figure for the child, with all else in the background. And from the child's responses the level and structure of intelligence could be determined.

There is another way of reading Binet that indicates how fragile the conceptual connections were in his mind between the child's behavior in the testing situation and his learning and behavior in other social milieus. Take, for example, the following statement by Binet and Simon (1916a):

> We believe that we have succeeded in completely disregarding the acquired information of the subject. We give him nothing to read, nothing to write, and submit him to no test in which he might succeed by means of rote learning. In fact we do not even notice his inability to read if a case occurs. It is simply the level of his natural intelligence that is taken into account. (P. 42)

It would be hard to find another statement that illustrates better an individual psychology. One can almost hear Binet's mind straining to blot out the possibility that what the child does in the testing situation is not independent of the child's place and experience in present and past social settings. The very phrase "natural intelligence," so Platonic and thinglike in its implications, stands in marked contrast (if not in contradiction) to the ways Binet talks about intelligence at other times. Although Binet knew better, a part of him had to believe that whatever he was "measuring" was not a consequence of factors outside the testing situation. What is ironic here is that although Binet was a vociferous opponent of the faculty psychology of his day, his imprisonment in that psychology showed up from time to time in his writings on intelligence.

If Binet took his own conceptions seriously, what would be some of the obvious features of the testing situation? One would be that it contains an adult and a child. Another would be that they are strangers to each other. A third feature would be that the surround is familiar to one and unfamiliar to the other. Another feature would be that the power relationships between the two people are very unequal. I do not mention these features to suggest that they play a role in the behavior of the two people. That suggestion requires no defense or elaboration. Indeed, since Binet's time there probably have been thousands of studies on "situational determinants" of individual behavior in testing situations. The purpose of these studies has been to make more valid assessments of an individual's performance and capabilities. All of these studies have asked: to what factors do we have to pay attention if we want to understand the substance and qualities of the interaction between two individuals? Although we have learned a lot from these studies, their emphasis on individuals and their interactions has effectively obscured issues that cast these interactions in a different light. For example, what if Binet had asked: "Why am I in a situation where I am testing children?" I assume that no one would be satisfied if Binet replied: "Because I want to be able to measure the developmental progression of the components of intelligence." We would feel somewhat more satisfied if he would reply: "The development of a scale of intelligence has very important theoretical and practical implications and if I am successful in my research I will be making a contribution to my science and my society." And then if we said to Binet:

> All well and good. You have told us what *you* are about but what I do not understand is what has made it possible for you to do what you are doing. Are you doing this on your own in the role of teacher and researcher, the way you have done so many things in the past? Even then you were not operating as a private individual but rather in a formal setting where you were expected to do what you were doing.

Wolf's (1973) biography of Binet tells us much about how Binet would have answered these questions. Central to the story is Binet's relationship to the Society for the Psychological Study of the Child:

> Binet also had the good fortune to be asked to join the newly founded *Société libre pour l'étude psychologique de l'enfant* hereafter referred to as *La Société*. This gave him both a "cause" to support and an opportunity to be allowed to go into the schools for his own experiments. *La Société* was founded to give teachers and school administrators an opportunity to meet to discuss problems of education and to be active participants in research investigations. It was exactly the sort of forum that Binet needed, for here he could press his ideas about the need for a union of education and psychology. He had hardly become a member before he emerged as the prime mover of the organization.
>
> It was not long before he persuaded the board of *La Société* to establish a publication, a *Bulletin,* which Binet edited. It provided a record of the so-called research carried out by the participant members, and of the monthly meetings that reveal Binet as a paternal and directing force. He cajoled and stimulated his *confrères,* guided and interpreted their studies, and infected them with his own enthusiasms and viewpoints. Members of this *Société* spearheaded the movement to arouse the Ministry of Public Instruction to do something on behalf of retarded schoolchildren. It was as leader of *La Société* that Binet was appointed to the famous study Commission from the vantage point of which he saw the compelling need to find a way to differentiate those children who could learn normally from those who could not. As a result, he and Simon forged the instruments that became in turn the 1905, 1908, and 1911 exemplars of the metric intelligence scale. (Pp. 21–22)

In the 1904 bulletin of the society, Binet announced the appointment of a ministerial commission for the abnormal by the French Ministry of Public Instruction (Wolf, 1973):

> We are happy to let our colleagues know of a very recent ministerial decision, proof that the questions to which our *Société* addresses itself are of highly practical interest, and also that the efforts made by our *Société* to bring about important reforms have not been useless. (P. 168)

He recalled that three members of the society had personally taken the resolution to the appropriate public administrators and added: "It is then with a profound satisfaction that we announce the decree by which M. Cahumie has just organized a commission charged with studying the question of abnormal children. This commission . . . counts among its members four of our colleagues [including Binet]'' (P. 168).

The degree to which Binet had become part of a political-professional-scientific-institutional network of relationships can be seen in the following description by Binet about the commission (Wolf, 1973):

> I cannot express the profound impression left on me of the memory of the ten months during which my colleagues, multiplying the meetings of the plenary commission and of the technical sub-commissions, the visits to the principal establishments of the abnormal, the consultations, and the examinations of notebooks, elucidated every day a point of the problem, and hastened the time when the solutions given for them could be translated into laws and regulations. (P. 168)

Although Binet fought the faculty psychology of the day, insofar as the social arrangements were concerned he did not grasp their unity or interrelationships. Administration, pedagogy, and science were for him distinct functions. That is to say, Binet saw himself as a scientist whose substantive concerns had no intrinsic relationships with these other functions (Wolf, 1973, p. 170). His task was to solve a scientific problem, which solution could then be applied by those with practical interests. And yet, as Wolf's biography demonstrates, the scientific and the practical were an indissoluble unity in Binet's experience. He always saw the scientific issue in the context of lives, institutions, and society. How else can one account for his efforts to attain a place in the social arrangements in order to change them? But Binet was quite conventional in his conception that the scientific and the practical are two distinct, basically unrelated areas. As a consequence, he could not entertain the possibility that by virtue of his theories, values, and place in the social order his work might not gain acceptance, i.e., that he was adversarially outside the educational culture and decisionmaking network. As Wolf notes, the appearance of his scale in France "raised scarcely a ripple. Even the Ministerial Commission seems to have been largely immune to it." It was not the first time that Binet's ideas and work did not receive acceptance, but he did not have a way of comprehending why these things happened except in terms of a psychology of individual personalities. Similarly, Binet's pleased response to the interests of American psychologists in his scales illustrates how conceptually insensitive he was to the question of why

American psychologists were so interested in his scales. To ask that question is to ask what were the features of American society, and the social place of these psychologists, that made his scales so attractive?

The outlines of the answer sketched above give one a very different view of Binet dealing with a child. That situation is not only an interpersonal interaction taking place in a limited geographical space. It is also a socially and officially sanctioned event reflecting the recognition of an undesirable state of affairs in a major social institution to which the larger society was becoming sensitive; moreover, it is an instance of a class of events intended to produce changes in that institution. Put in another way, Binet with a child testifies to an ongoing change in a public policy, a change that is explicitly supposed to alter the structure of schools. And Binet has become a willing part of that change process; he is an agent of that policy. More than that, he has put himself into a formal relationship with the structures of institutions that are the object of change. Binet with a child is an individual but if we want to understand why he is with the child we obviously get a very incomplete answer if we observe him only with the child. We can film and record the interaction and come up with fascinating and important behavioral regularities but we find out little about why Binet is with the child. We could intuit some answers but they would largely be in terms of that particular interaction.

What I am suggesting, of course, is that for us who are watching such an interaction there are (or could be) two types of ground: one is immediately perceptible in that circumscribed space. That is to say, Binet and the child are figure and all other objects and characteristics in that space are ground. But there is another type of ground that is not perceptible, which for the moment I shall call the social arrangements without which we can understand Binet with a child in only very limited ways. By social arrangements I refer to an amalgam of the formal contacts and agreements Binet has with individuals and institutions in regard to his work; the ways in which these agreements on purposes vary as a function of the individual's formal role in relation to institutional policy formation and decisionmaking; the changing (or unchanging) nature of power relationships within and between institutions and agencies, i.e., the network of relationships within which Binet is formally and informally embedded; and the points of contact between all of the above and the political system.

There is a more simple and general way of talking about social arrangements: Binet, like every other human being, lives in a highly structured social milieu the rules and traditions of which govern, formally and informally, the transactions between individuals and among groups and social institutions; these rules and traditions may be more or less honored in practice, they may change over time, and their significance for the uses and distribution of power becomes most clear when these rules and traditions are under pressure to change. People (like Binet) may be unaware of many of these rules and traditions and, therefore, be insensitive to the basis for the milieu's organization. But when these rules and traditions are subject to change, people become aware that their milieu, far from being a random ordering of individuals, groups, and institutions, has ordered meanings and design. At such times, what was for people ground becomes figure, and because individuals, groups, and institutions perceive that changes in the heretofore unreflectively accepted order will have differential consequences for their place in the milieu, they will take different stances toward change.

So, from one standpoint we can explain Binet with a child in interpersonal terms, which reduces to a psychology of interacting individuals. If we knew what was "in" Binet's mind and that of the child we would be in a position to explain the behavioral regularities of the interaction, although our major interest, as that of Binet, would center on the child. In fact, it would seem self-evident to most people that the interaction is taking place because Binet wants to learn something about that individual child. But from another standpoint the fact that Binet is in that type of situation can be explained in terms of the relationships Binet has in an ordered milieu of individuals, groups, and institutions. The two standpoints are not antithetical. In fact, they share two axioms: the data or observations relevant to each standpoint have a comprehensible order and the figure-ground relationships in the order will vary as a function of the observer's purposes and conceptual framework. As I shall be arguing later, there is a third axiom: in the world of human social affairs the two standpoints are part of a single order. If for our different purposes we say that there are two standpoints, let us recognize that we do so for *our* special purposes and not because the social realities are organized as if there were two standpoints. From Wolf's biography of Binet there is evidence that he knew there were the two standpoints but there is no doubt that Binet was far more sophisticated about how to think about and study individuals than he was about how his work would be perceived and utilized by different individuals and institutions in the network of relationships in which he was embedded. Phenomenologically, he knew that his studies of individual children already reflected a change in attitude among members of that network, and it was his earnest hope that his studies would produce other changes in the structure and practices of schools, but this knowledge could not be integrated by Binet into his psychological theorizing. Binet's psychological theorizing, as well as the research to which it gave rise, centered around the development of an individual's intelligence. In that kind of theorizing there was no place for incorporating what I have called the second standpoint (or the social arrangements.)

Two arguments can be made against my position, although they are variations on a single theme. The first argument is that what I would have hoped Binet would have incorporated into his systematic thinking is not really psychology. It may be important—a lot of things are important, but that does not mean that they should be encompassed in any major way within psychological theory. After all, the argument would be, psychological theory has enough trouble dealing with relatively circumscribed issues of human behavior and development, without grandiosely taking on other issues that are tangentially psychological. There are several ways in which this argument can be countered but the one I will employ here brings us back to the earlier question: why is *Binet* with a child? I put the question thus precisely because we have evidence that Binet was aware of the multiple sources that combined to put him in the room with a child, just as he was also aware of the ramifications he hoped his work would have. If his awareness was not of a depth and clarity to allow him to encompass these factors in his theorizing, that is no warrant for concluding they are not crucial for understanding Binet.

What I am saying to be psychologically true for Binet is true for every human being. Each of us is an individual whose thinking and overt behavior have been shaped—not in a vacuum or in randomly ordered social arrangements. Although we may not be aware of this fact, it nevertheless has an important role in the theories of psychologists. But Binet was aware of the issue because he saw the individual child's behavior in terms of ordered milieus outside the testing situation. He was not content with merely observing and recording a child's behavior in the testing situation. He knew the child had a family, was in a school, and came from a particular social stratum and geographical district. Binet deeply believed that intelligence is "educable" and that belief rested on the assumption that the reordering of milieus could have major effects on the individual's functioning. Whether, or to what extent, that assumption is valid is still controversial but that should not obscure the fact that no psychologist, beginning with Binet, would disagree with what he said should be taken into account in understanding a child. *What I have been contending is that what is central for understanding the child is no less central for understanding Binet.* I would argue that given Binet's hope to effect changes in the schools, his failure to see his place in the network of ordered relationships into which his own efforts had catapulted him would ultimately defeat him. He was playing for high stakes but he did not understand the game of social dynamics within and among the groups and institutions to which he and his hopes were tied.

The second argument is that I am being unfair in hoping that Binet would have seen the issue as I do. Binet was a developmental psychologist and I am disappointed that he was not also a social psychologist. Is that not asking too much? One could interpret this argument as conceding the point that by focusing on individual children Binet could not see the possible consequences for his work arising from his relationship to and understanding of the network of groups and institutions of which he was a part. The unhappy fact is that neither then nor now has social psychology dealt with the issue I have raised. American social psychology has not in any of its major theorizings taken seriously the psychologist's place in the social arrangements and the bearing that place has on what happens to him or her as a person as well as on the social consequences of the psychologist's work. The issue is not in whose domain the problem belongs. It is a central question for every kind of psychologist because every psychologist's thinking and work bear the imprint of his or her place in the social arrangements. And the consequences that work may have always bear the imprint of those social arrangements. What is true for the psychologist is no less true for the individuals he or she studies. To act, let alone theorize, as if that were not the case is tantamount to assuming that we are born into, grow up in, and live our lives in randomly ordered milieus. We know that is patently false. I daresay that hardly an hour goes by when we are not made aware that our feelings, thoughts, and actions affect and are affected by characteristics of ordered milieus. Why this obvious fact has not been central to psychology we shall take up later. Let us now turn to the consequences of Binet's thinking and work for the light they shed on what happens when this obvious fact is not taken seriously.

Although I said earlier that there is a fragile conceptual tie in Binet's theorizing between his view of the measurement of intelligence in an individual testing situation and the milieus in which the child lives, it is nevertheless remarkable the degree to which Binet was sensitive to the fact that milieus are ordered and that societies differ in how they are ordered. As Wolf (1973) rightly notes:

> Even as early as 1896 [Binet] was seeking ways to determine "the organization of intellectual functions in different cultural milieus, including national cultures, [and] socioeconomic levels." He also sought to know what might be the effects of "typical problem-solving styles . . . or response styles" on mental organization when in 1903 he made the masterful study of his daughters' habitual orientations of thought. Furthermore, his certainties about the pervasive nature of the emotions on intellectual acts can be translated into the current belief that "the separations between abilities and personality traits is artificial and the two domains need to be rejoined in interpreting an individual's test scores." His penchant for improvement strongly suggests that he would have deplored "the built-in inertia of tests," perhaps especially of his own. Indeed, the fact that so many of his ideas emerge as important problems a half-century after his death underlines the unhappy conclusion that his disciples often failed to appreciate, perhaps even to understand, the real bases for Binet's psychological methods and thought. (Pp. 217–218)

Binet had a generalizing type of mind, bringing factors into relationships with each other that most psychologists kept apart; that is, he tended to see wholes where other people saw elements. He was not content in establishing that individuals differ but sought also to demonstrate why they differ and the implications of the answer for "improvement." Wolf is absolutely correct in concluding that those who came after Binet seized on his methods and not on his thinking. But in one respect Binet was like the psychologists who came after him: he and they wanted to have some effect on their society but had no real conceptual framework with which to understand their society and their place in it.

Binet's early death robs us of an answer to an intriguing question: how would he have reacted to the consequences (national and interna-

tional) of his work? Would he have been aghast, as Wolf suggests, at
how society has made use of his work? All we know is that his plans
centered around determining "the law of the intellectual development
of children and [devising] a method of measuring their intelligence;
and, second, [studying] the diversity of their intellectual aptitudes"
(Binet and Simon, 1916a, p. 42). These are not the words of a person
disposed to see himself, his theories, and his work in terms of their
societal antecedents and consequences. They are the words of a person
of his time: one individual seeking to understand the behavior of other
individuals. They are the words of a person with a world view that
prevented him from recognizing that his concept of intelligence was an
invention and, like all inventions, as revealing of the inventor's society
as of the inventor: intelligence, as an invented concept, in the ways we
define and use it, was created in a particular era of Western society.
The idea that intelligence is measurable and the idea that it *should* be
measured were not matters of either personal esthetics or scientific
necessity but outcroppings from societal transformations initiated by
the American and French revolutions, each in its own way influencing
and changing power relationships within countries, radically redefin-
ing traditional conceptions of the relationship between human performance and status, setting into motion vast immigrations, providing a
rationale for the benefits of education, and culminating in the nineteenth century in universal compulsory education.

To Binet, his theorizing had roots in his research, and in the
research and theories of others, but not in the world view he had
assimilated in his socialization. Indeed, as I indicated earlier, Binet's
world view was subject (in principle) to every criticism he had made of
the faculty psychology of his day. As best as I can tell, Binet saw his
society as a congeries of "elements," and he evinced no interest in
understanding their significance and possible relationships. Society
was out there—not in every part of his being (and, therefore, his
theories); understanding reality would come via commitment to
science, not by flushing out how people assimilate and are circumscribed by a world view that defines reality for you long before you
experience it. So, it is not surprising that Binet was not at all sensitive
to such questions as the following: why, in contrast to earlier times, are
so many people in *Western* societies writing about and doing research
on *intelligence?* Why are so many of these investigators predisposed to
come up with a definition and measurement that could and should be

used by the larger society? In light of what is (or could have been) known about *industrializing* Western societies, what functions would the measurement of intelligence serve in those societies? Is it conceivable, and from what standpoint, that the measurement of intelligence would cause harm, perhaps more harm than good? It is the last question that is the most fateful because when people (like psychologists) seek to give to society a means that it says it needs to solve a problem, the very bases (ideological, political, economic, religious, ethnic) on which that society is organized constitute an obstacle to asking, let alone answering, the question. And precisely because the psychologist has been socialized into his or her society, has assimilated a world view peculiar to that society, and occupies a special niche in the social order, the question of whose oxen will be gored by the psychologist's theories and research, and the social actions they give rise to, is likely to be answered in societally self-serving ways.

What happened to Binet's work is as clear a picture as one can find of how traditions, values, and social structural characteristics can transform, shape, and direct the course of ideas and technical innovations. It is also an instance of how unaware psychologists were of how effectively socialized they had been, a socialization that had given them a world view in which the possibility that they might do harm was literally unthinkable. The story is a long, complicated, and fascinating one that has been described elsewhere (Sarason and Doris, 1969, 1979) and I shall present only some of the highlights, paying particular attention to our own society.

The alacrity with which Binet's scales were taken over and applied in our country in the early decades of this century has to be seen in terms of three overriding societal concerns or beliefs: "feeble-mindedness" was assumed to be a major factor in the cause of delinquency, crime, prostitution, venereal disease, illegitimacy, alcoholism, and poverty; immigration would have profoundly adverse effects on the social order; and, with the advent of universal compulsory education, schools were faced with mammoth educational, organizational, and social tasks. But *who* had these concerns and why were these people in positions to proclaim them and to make them a basis for public policy and legislation? The answer, in brief, is that these people were not a random sample of the population. They were not Catholics, Jews, or blacks. They were not poor people. They were not uneducated. They were not without access to elective office, public forums, and communications media. And they were not people indifferent to how society was and should be ordered. Indeed, these people had an acute sense not only of the society's need to be ordered but also of the interrelationships in that order, i.e., how things worked, where power resided, and how things got done. I am not here arguing from a Marxist perspective but simply noting that the society was comprised of different religious, ethnic, and socioeconomic groups very much aware of each other and varying in their relationships to political power and in their perspectives on social traditions. The people most articulate about the three societal concerns did not, of course, see themselves as prejudiced or self-serving or antidemocratic. They saw themselves as individual agents of progress stemming the forces that would subvert that progress. They may have been businessmen, clergymen, elected officials, or university professors but they would deny that their concerns as individuals were determined other than by facts and obvious "truths." Indeed, there has long been in our society a tradition of denying that where you are in the social order is a potent factor in how you think and what you value.*

It is not fortuitous, of course, that the people voicing these concerns seized on Binet's work as a means to prove their worst fears and to push for remedial action. These means were provided by some noted American psychologists (Goddard, Terman, Kuhlmann, and Pintner) who adapted or "improved" Binet's scales for use in this country. Like Binet they focused primarily on the development of a more reliable and valid test of an individual's intelligence. They, like Binet, saw themselves as individuals contributing to their field as well as providing their society with a more rational basis for dealing with its problems. And the scientific contributions they hoped to make would illuminate and, they hoped, solve problems of great significance to other scientific fields, e.g., biology and eugenics, where the nature of racial differences, especially intellectual, was a major focus. To understand the scientific and social implications of these interrelationships, and how they bear on the present discussion, a bit of history is required.

In discussing the relationship of racism and imperialism in

* This denial has been one of the most effective bulwarks for a psychology of the individual because it renders it unnecessary for the psychologist to ask how his thinking and work are related to his place in the social order and how the uses to which he or others put his work reflect his relationship to that order.

America about the turn of the century, Hofstadter (1959) makes the point that the Anglo-Saxon form of racism then prevalent was basically a product of modern nationalism and the romantic movement. To be sure, it derived strong support from Darwinism, which with its leitmotif of struggle and survival of the fittest provided vivid analogies and "scientific" support to the proponents of racial superiority and aggressive international politics. While Anglo-Saxonism saw the international scene as a struggle for survival among nations and races and hence generally supported American imperialism in the decades before World War I, there were nevertheless those among the Anglo-Saxon enthusiasts who strongly deplored warfare for its dysgenic effect. Such was Henry Fairfield Osborn, distinguished paleontologist and eugenicist, who saw in the Great War the destruction of the best of American stock. Emotionally moved by his observations of the mobilization of troops, he commented (Osborn, 1919):

> Whatever may be its intellectual, its literary, its artistic or its musical aptitudes, as compared with other races, the Anglo-Saxon branch of the Nordic race is again showing itself to be that upon which the nation must chiefly depend for leadership, for courage, for loyalty, for unity and harmony of action, for self-sacrifice and devotion to an ideal. Not that members of other races are not doing their part, many of them are, but in no other human stock which has come to this country is there displayed the unanimity of heart, mind and action which is now being displayed by the descendants of the blue-eyed, fair-haired peoples of the north of Europe. In a recent journey in northern California and Oregon I noted that, in the faces of the regiments which were first to leave for the city of New York and later that, in the wonderful array of young men at Plattsburg, the Anglo-Saxon type was clearly dominant over every other and the purest members of this type largely outnumbered the others. . . . With a race having these predispositions, extending back to the very beginnings of European history, there is no hesitation or even waiting for conscription and the sad thought was continually in my mind in California, in Oregon and in Plattsburg that again this race was passing, that this war will take a very heavy toll of this strain of Anglo-Saxon life which has played so large a part in American history. (Pp. xi–xiii)

"Scientific" support for racism began with Galton, the founder of the eugenics movement. Although he was apparently not guilty of racial animosity as such, he nevertheless felt that the theory of evolution and the available evidence led inevitably to the conclusion that various human races differed not only in physical characteristics but also in intellectual and behavioral traits. In *Hereditary Genius* (1869) Galton attempted to demonstrate the existence of these differences. His principal argument was based upon estimations of the frequency with which men of genius had been produced by different races. Thus, with complete obliviousness to cultural, historical, and environmental factors he estimated that the Anglo-Saxon race was superior to the black and the black to the Australian aborigine. Unlike many other racists, however, Galton was broad-minded enough, and objective enough, within the limits of his science, to allow that another race might be superior to his own. Thus, relying on the frequency of eminent men in the golden age of Athens he argued that

> the average ability of the Athenian race is, on the lowest possible estimate, very nearly two grades higher than our own—that is, about as much as our race is above that of the African negro. This estimate, which may seem prodigious to some, is confirmed by the quick intelligence and high culture of the Athenian commonalty, before whom literary works were recited, and works of art exhibited, of a far more severe character than could possibly be appreciated by the average of our race, the calibre of whose intellect is easily gauged by a glance at the contents of a railway book-stall. (P. 342)

While it would appear that Galton's argument for racial differences in intellect and personality was derived in part from or at least conditioned by evolutionary theory, the hypothesis—and the racist attitudes that so often accompany it—is of course at least as old as recorded history, and it may be presumed that whatever objective evidence exists for the hypothesis, the accompanying racist attitudes derive from and are supported by primitive and widely prevalent psychic needs of both individuals and social groups. Thus, we interpret Hofstadter's indictment of modern nationalism and the romantic movement as causes of racism to refer to the particular form that racism took during this period of modern history. At any rate, there would appear to be no question, as Hofstadter and others have documented, that the aggressive and expansionist international politics of the United States around the turn of the century received strong support from the world view of Anglo-Saxonism.

If on the international scene Anglo-Saxonism was concerned with bearing the white man's burden and spreading the benefits of Anglo-

Saxon civilization, on the domestic scene it joined with other variants of racism then prevalent in a concern for preserving the purity of the breed. The growing racist attitudes in America in the latter part of the nineteenth century were expressed in the increasing demand for immigration restrictions, which would preserve the blood of the old immigrant stock from northern Europe—the blood that had founded this country and made it great (Haller, 1963). The increasing flood of immigrants from southern and eastern Europe, with its alien Catholic and Jewish religions, foreign folkways, and strange tongues, alarmed a native population under stress because of the rapid social and economic changes that followed the Civil War. Spokesmen readily appeared for the racist attitudes that emerged in this period of strain, and in 1894 a group of young Harvard graduates formed the Immigration Restriction League.

The development of the eugenics movement in this country provided these advocates of racial exclusiveness with another outlet for their propaganda and one that smacked of scientific respectability. In 1911, Prescott Hall, a leader of the Immigration Restriction League, in conjunction with his old Harvard classmate Charles Davenport, arranged to have a committee on immigration attached to the eugenics section of the American Breeders Association. The first report of the committee appeared in the *American Breeders Magazine* the following year. The report advocated more rigorous enforcement of existing restrictions on the admission of the alien insane and feebleminded, along with extension of these regulations. The feebleminded were viewed as perhaps an even greater menace to public health than the insane, for the latter were more likely to be segregated in institutions. But great as the danger was from classifiable defectives it was seen as "less than the danger from the much larger class of aliens who are below the mental and physical average of their own countries and cannot fail to lower the average here" (Cance, Field, Ward, and Hall, 1912, p. 252).*

*Franz Boas dissented from the conclusions and recommendations of the committee on immigration and subsequently resigned. This dean of American anthropologists and longtime critic of racism surely must have found himself among strange bedfellows. He was replaced by Irving Fisher, a Yale economist and a leading eugenicist. With the transformation of the American Breeders Association into the American Genetic Association, the reports of this committee on immigration subsequently appeared in that association's official organ, the *Journal of Heredity,* and they continued to advocate restrictive immigration policies.

While Galton's argument for racial differences in intellectual ability was circuitous, the development of intelligence tests appeared to give a means for a direct comparison of racial and ethnic groups. Goddard (1913) was one of the first to apply Binet tests to immigrant groups, with the intent of determining whether methods for keeping out defective aliens could be improved. In reporting on his experiences at Ellis Island he notes the "uncanny" ability of one of his fieldworkers for identifying the feebleminded:

> We picked out one young man whom we suspected was defective, and, through the interpreter, proceeded to give him the test. The boy tested eight by the Binet scale. The interpreter said, "I could not have done that when I came to this country," and seemed to think the test unfair. We convinced him that the boy was defective. That was so impressive that the Commissioner urged us to come back on the following Monday. We did, spending the day there and trying some experiments. We placed one young lady at the end of the line, and as the immigrants passed, she pointed out the ones she thought defective. They were taken to the quiet room, and we proceeded to test them. She picked out nine, whom she thought were defective. The result was that every one of the nine were below normal, according to the Binet test. (P. 105)

This work was continued and reported in full in a 1917 issue of the *Journal of Delinquency*. In this report six groups of steerage passengers were selected from the immigrants at Ellis Island. They were chosen only after the physicians of the immigration service had culled out all the mental defectives that they recognized as such. Two of the groups, one Italian and the other Russian, had been selected by one of Goddard's fieldworkers as appearing defective. Out of a combined total of thirty-seven in these two groups only one achieved as high a classification as borderline on the Binet; the remainder were either morons or imbeciles. The other four groups—Jews, Hungarians, Italians, and Russians—were selected as representative of steerage passengers in general but to compensate for the fact that the immigration authorities had already removed the obviously mentally defective from among the passengers, Goddard excluded from his groups a small but unspecified number of obviously intelligent immigrants. In the resulting select but "representative" samples the Binet tests revealed an average of 80 percent feebleminded immigrants.

Apparently embarrassed by riches, Goddard removed some of the test items that had proved most difficult for the immigrant groups and rescored the tests. But even with this liberal treatment approximately 40 percent of each group proved feebleminded, failing to achieve a mental age score of ten years or better. Not only were these results true for the immigrant groups for which it had been necessary to use a translator in the administration of the tests but they held as well for the Jewish group, for which it was possible to use an examiner who spoke the language of the group.

Presenting these results, Goddard (1917) then addresses himself to the skeptical reader:

> Doubtless the thought in every reader's mind is the same as in ours, that it is impossible that half of such a group of immigrants could be feebleminded, but we know that it is never wise to discard a scientific result because of apparent absurdity. Many a scientific discovery has seemed at first glance absurd. We can only arrive at the truth by fairly and conscientiously analyzing the data. (P. 266)

First, Goddard points out that the immigration of recent years is inferior in quality to that of the past: "It is admitted on all sides that we are getting now the poorest of each race." Second, Goddard points out that the great majority of these feebleminded immigrants belong to the moron class, a class capable of earning a living under favorable circumstances. These favorable circumstances according to Goddard usually existed for the immigrant:

> He is watched and protected because he does not know the customs of the country. He is excused because he does not understand the language. His every act and movement is more or less closely supervised because he is a foreigner. In a large percentage of the cases he goes at once, when he lands, to his own group. They protect and care for him, partly through racial pride, partly through common humanity, extending to him the care and oversight and patience which we have just mentioned. (P. 268)

Thus the moron immigrant is capable of succeeding after a fashion in the New World and our average citizen, who is likely to have contact with only the more successful and prosperous of the immigrant stock, would on the basis of his limited experience easily underestimate the surprisingly large percentage of immigrants who are of relatively low mentality.

During this period around World War I there were numerous additional applications of the Binet and other newly developed tests of intelligence to the study of ethnic and racial groups. Rather than pursue further individual examples of this kind of research, appreciation can be gained of the way in which this research appeared to an expert in the field and the way it was presented to students by looking at one of the early, outstanding college textbooks in the area of intelligence testing. Rudolph Pintner, a professor of education at Columbia University, published his text in 1923. He was then in full stride in a distinguished career marked by many contributions to the testing movement, including such special tests as the Pintner-Patterson Performance Test and the Pintner Non-Language Test (with which he pioneered in the application of intelligence tests to deaf children).

In his review of the use of intelligence tests with various "racial groups" in America Pintner reports on six studies of Italian children in which median Binet IQs ranged from 77.5 to 85. For three comparison groups of children of "native" American stock the median IQs ranged from 95 to 106. Pintner discusses briefly the variables of social status and language in these studies but concludes that although the median IQ of the Italian in the United States might not be as low as indicated by the results it was probably still below 100. In discussing Binet test results on other ethnic groups he urges caution since the data were not as extensive as those available on the Italian groups but reasons that perhaps the groups coming from southern Europe were inferior in intelligence to those of northern Europe. This point, of course, although Pintner does not mention it, would support the then prevalent racist belief in the superiority of Nordic blood.

Pintner then refers to the results of the U.S. Army testing program in World War I and indicates that they also give support for the assumption of a superiority of the northern European over the southern or eastern European. In his concluding remarks on these ethnic groups Pintner carefully notes that the results are indicative of differences in these groups as they are represented in this country and points out a need for comparisons among "races" in their home countries.

As regards the American black, Pintner presents three Binet studies comparing black and white school children. The median IQs for the black groups ranged from 7 to 24 points below those of the white groups. There is no discussion of educational, cultural, or socioeconomic factors that might concomitantly vary with the racial groupings. Another study discussed by Pintner compared a group of black and white children in terms of the mental age obtained on the Goddard revision. Approximately 30 percent of the black children were more retarded even when compared with "poor whites" as represented by the children of mill workers. A final Binet study compared black college students with white college students. The fifty-five black students obtained a median IQ of 103 and the seventy-five white students a median IQ of 112. Pintner further discusses the testing of black and white soldiers in World War I and concludes that all results show the black decidedly inferior to the white on standard intelligence tests.

Thus results of approximately a decade of research on the question of racial and ethnic differences in intelligence appeared to an expert and were so presented to his students in one of the outstanding schools of education in this country. We need not follow the story of how the intelligence test results of the army recruits in World War I were used to keep the fires of conflict and prejudice blazing and to give impetus to discriminatory legislation. I have given enough of the story to illustrate several points.

1. Distinguished psychologists, influenced by Binet, saw the measurement of intelligence as a significant scientific achievement.

2. These psychologists understood well that this achievement would and should have practical social significance.

3. Although their scientific achievement was in measuring individual intelligence, they used these tests (as did others) as a way of coming to conclusions about groups of people viewed pejoratively by more forceful segments of the social order.

4. There is no evidence that as a group these psychologists differed in attitude from these more powerful segments; on the contrary, there is evidence that they became interrelated with them and in effect were willing agents of that part of the social order. In their writings and public pronouncements they may not have used the florid, exhortatory, and inflammatory language of some public figures but they shared a number of concerns.

5. These psychologists were unable to ask and pursue the following question: in what ways and to what extent is the *substance* of my thinking and research related to who I am and where I am in the social scheme of things? After all, they could have said, my thinking and research are not about sticks and stones but about people of whom I am one instance. Are my theories and research independent of where I

am in a complex but ordered network of relationships? Are my explicit
theories devoid of any implicit view of what makes people tick, how
they become what they are, and what accounts for their view of their
social world?

The last point is, of course, the crucial one for my argument
because the inability of these psychologists to ask and pursue these
questions insured that their theories and research would play into and
reinforce the prejudiced attitudes of the dominant groups in the society, groups to which these psychologists belonged. And in so belonging
they were part of the social force that formulated and helped achieve
legal sanction for public policies that adversely affected large segments
of the population. Their theories were about individuals, not about the
nature and workings of ordered milieus into which people are born
and live. They were theories about the complexities of the individual
mind, not about the complexities of the individual's ordered milieu.
Of course, they knew that society was ordered and that there was order
in every individual's milieu. And of course they knew that there were
great differences among milieus in terms of the bases on which they
were ordered. They knew perfectly well that no individual lives in a
randomly ordered milieu. But for these psychologists the fascinating
problem was understanding the individual mind for the complexity of
which they had the highest respect. The theoretical puzzle was in that
individual mind. *The social order was not a puzzle, it was a given and
therefore could be ground and the individual mind figure. What their stance could
not permit them to see was that they had such a respect for the social order, such a
stake in preserving it as they knew it, that they could not distance themselves from
it.* It was, to use Murray Levine's felicitous phrase, the triumph in
theory and research of "intrapsychic supremacy."

Phenomenologically, psychologists saw their theories as their personal creation, building on whatever knowledge their science provided
them. It is instructive (but ironic) that the psychologists understood
well that their theories and research were very much shaped by their
belonging to a professional-scientific order; that is, they were in
departments of psychology, they were members of regional and national professional or scientific societies, they wrote for psychology
journals, they helped edit them, and they trained the new generation
of psychologists. That kind of social order they comprehended and
would have accorded a role in shaping their theories and research.
And they also would have readily acknowledged that they were part of

and influenced by a larger order of scientists. In that sense these psychologists recognized that as individuals they had been and would continue to be influenced in their theorizing and research by the traditions, values, and conceptions of a particular segment of the social order. What they could not pursue and, therefore, recognize as additional determinants of their theories and research was that they were part of other segments of the social order. They were, for example, *Americans* and all that signifies about implicit and explicit traditions, world outlook, right and wrong ways of living, and the meaning of patriotism. It never could occur to them that their theories of individuals might not be unrelated to a virtue that had long been revered in this country: rugged individualism. Although they knew that the constitution kept church and state apart, there is no evidence that they appreciated the degree to which our political system was largely dominated by certain groups in certain churches. And the same held in regard to business, finance, and industry. Nor did they understand (or if they understood, had questions about) how their colleges and universities were related to, and the degree to which they were controlled by, highly selective, frequently interrelated samples of the religious, political, business-finance-industry populations.

Each of these psychologists would have hooted at the accusation that they had two psychologies: one for themselves and one for people in general. But if they would have given short shrift to such criticism, they never seemed to be able to ask how the substance of their psychology derived from transactions in their lives between idiosyncratic and social order factors. They could not entertain the possibility that although their theories were about individuals, these theories were not asocial in derivation and, therefore, had to be examined to see how they reflected the weltanschauung of those parts of the social order to which these psychologists belonged. So, for example, they knew that their interest in a theory of intelligence stemmed in part from their society's definition of, explanation of, and concern about "social problems," but they were unable to see that their conceptualizations of intelligence could, explicitly and implicitly, be a reflection of some of the features of that society. They could understand that these conceptualizations might be viewed rather differently by people in parts of the social order quite different from their own, but that signified that these people lacked the conceptual tools to be objective and analytical.

In referring to these early distinguished psychologists I have no intention of maligning them. They, like we, were social beings embedded in the social matrix of their times, a highly ordered matrix in which they occupied certain roles highly correlated with education, social power, religion, access to public forums, and certain societal ideals and beliefs deriving from an identification with national history and traditions. They, like we, were far more aware of how they hoped to make an impact on their society than they were of the ways in which the substance of the psychologizing informing their actions in part reflected their place in the social order. This is not to say, of course, that the theoretical and methodological problems with which they were occupied were unimportant and that the contributions they made were trivial. What I am saying is that the formulation of these problems was not independent of their place in the social order and that the adverse social consequences of these formulations derived in part from the place these psychologists occupied in the social order. They had the highest hopes that their new science would make for a better society but the complexities and order of that society had no formal place in their psychology of individuals. The mysteries that intrigued them were in the human mind. That was figure; all else was background. They had learned a great deal from their perceptual studies of individuals about reversing figure and ground and some of the illusory qualities of figure and ground relationships. But those principles and knowledge could not be applied to the individual-social order figure-ground relationship.

The point I am emphasizing is one that explains why biography is so interesting and instructive. The best biographers have a decided advantage over their subjects in that they are better situated to see relationships between the subject and his or her times and larger social context. The biographer seeks to make sense of the workings of the subject's mind but he or she is not content with what the person said, wrote, or did—or even with what other people said the person said, did, or wrote. What the biographer goes on to do is to describe the possible relationships between overt and covert behavior, on the one hand, and the ordered milieus experienced by the subject in his or her lifetime, on the other hand. And the best biographers attempt to discern how the characteristics of these ordered milieus have to be seen in terms of the features of the larger society. It is as if the axiom of these biographers is that the substance and structure of an individual—the warf and woof of the content and style of his or her thinking and actions—cannot be understood in terms of a narrow psychology of the individual. The subject is generally center stage but the biographer makes us aware (as often the subject was not) that the setting of that stage is always exerting an influence, sometimes subtle and sometimes blatant. Often the subject is not center stage because the biographer, by reversing figure and ground, wants us to discern that the relations between figure and ground are not passive. And if these relations are so complex that the subject may be only dimly or not at all aware of them, it is also true that some of these relations escape the biographer, which is why subsequent biographers try their hand at a new version of the subject's life and times. The worst biographers are those who are unaware that *their* perspective on the biographee is not independent of their place in the social order. Insensitive to the forces that shaped their own perspective, they cannot be expected to do justice to the forces that shaped that of the biographee. And, let us note, the reason why "authorized" or "house biographies" are suspect is the knowledge that because of the relationship between the biographer and the authorizers the probability of distortion and special dealing is extraordinarily high. In the case of psychologists and biographers the content of one's thinking is a function, among other things, of what you know and who and where you are in the social order.

From today's vantage point we know that the early theorizers about intelligence were quite unaware of the complexities of the issues. Scarr (1978) has put it well in an article with the arresting title "From Evaluation to Larry P., or What Shall We Do about IQ Tests?"

> IQ tests are a dilemma in that great morality play, "Who Shall Enjoy Society's Privileges?" Legal authorities battle over IQ tests as heroes or villains. The stages are courts around the nation, jammed with plaintiffs whose test scores were used to reject them from desired educational and occupational positions or whose scores exceeded those of others who were selected for desired positions on non-intellective bases. Larry P., Bakke, and Griggs are but a few of the plaintiffs whose names may become household words in the late '70s. Judges know little about the technical construction of IQ tests, their appropriate use and interpretation, and about the underlying issues of inequality that bring the adversaries to court. But the judges will decide how, when, and for whom IQ tests may be used to make life decisions.

As in most decisions in which morality plays an important role, there is conflicting "evidence" from the scientific community about the meaning, value, validity, and most of all, *legitimacy* of IQ measures. The history of IQ tests, for example, can be told as one of psychology's greatest achievements . . . or as one of its most shameful. . . . Proponents of the use of IQ tests cite their exemplary statistical virtues, opponents strike at their role in perpetuating social and economic injustice. If the experts line up in support of or against IQ tests, as physicians stand up for antibiotics and against VD, there would be no moral dilemma. It is the absence of scientific consensus that leaves IQ tests at the doubtful mercy of the legal system.

If the experts are so divided, as they were not at the turn of the century, it is in part because they take such different views of how one's place in the social order shapes the style and substance of intellectual functioning and, no less important, they differ in their willingness to examine how psychological theories are not independent of where the theorist sees himself or herself in the social order. From one standpoint the psychologists participating in the "great morality play" occupy similar places in the social order by virtue of education, position, and socioeconomic status. But unlike the early psychologists they vary considerably in political orientation, ethnic and racial background, and religious affiliation. It is not fortuitous that one of the most incisive critiques of IQ tests was made by Allison Davis in 1951, presented as the Inglis lectures at Harvard. From reading the book, *Social-Class Influences upon Learning,* one would never know that Davis was black. However, as soon as one knows this fact one understands why the substance of Davis's thinking cannot be understood in terms of an individual psychology disengaged from the context of place in the social order. There is a part of us that has been schooled to separate the substance of a psychological theory from the theorist as a person embedded in the social order. We have been taught that adherence to the canons, morality, and methods of science requires that separation be both possible and necessary. And, indeed, the way we write up our investigations and theories is intended to convince the reader that who we are and where we are in the social order are of no moment to the reader.

Psychologists do not enter the scientific arena with a blank mind. Willy-nilly, they were psychologists before they became psychologists: they had "theories" about what moves people, why people differ, what actions are "better" than other actions, how society is organized and why it should change or remain the same, and that although "luck" is a factor in living one has to proceed as though society, far from being a random affair, is sufficiently ordered so as to require one to learn how to use that order for one's purposes. Formal education as a psychologist changes one insofar as one is taught a new language, helps to unlearn what one knew as an "amateur" psychologist, and exposes one to new ways of thinking about, studying, and altering the behavior of people. But one thing does not change: the stuff of one's thinking, imaginings, and ruminations is people. (I have never known an animal psychologist who denied that his thinking about the behavior of the animal he was studying was devoid of human qualities.) More than that, thinking about other people always bears the imprint of how one views oneself, and although that view may contain idiosyncratic features it also contains features of one's experiences and place in the social order. As psychologists we would like to believe that we transcend or control for these features but that is and always has been a delusion, one that too frequently has been self-defeating for the psychologist and harmful to others.

Among the several major contributions of Freud was his recognition of some of the deeply personal obstacles inevitably standing in the way of one person understanding another. He thought that these obstacles could in large measure be circumvented by requiring the analyst, through personal analysis, to experience the validity of Freud's formulations, i.e., to see in his own development those processes and experiences he would seek to help others uncover in their development. This expectation foundered, however, on the phenomenon of countertransference. However successful the analyst's personal analysis may be, however insightful he may be about the dynamics of his patients, the very nature of the ordered relationship between analyst and client (doctor-patient, superior-inferior, payer-payee, rule setter–rule follower) will elicit in each, in a profoundly personal way, the forces that set definite limits on mutual comprehension. When, toward the end of his long life, Freud recommended that analysts be reanalyzed every five years, it was a measure of the deep respect he had for the limits of people's capacity to transcend subjectivity. Renewed self-knowledge would be helpful but the problem was inherently unresolvable.

In his own way Freud was a psychologist of the individual mind. It is true, of course, that he brilliantly illuminated the dynamics of family relationships and to that extent showed that where one is and who one is in the *familial* order are fateful for how one views self and others. But Freud never pursued the possibility that the seamless psychological web in which he viewed individual and family is part of a larger, highly differentiated, ordered social web. Ironically, Freud was very much aware (as a Jew in Catholic Austria) of this point but he presented his theories as though it did not matter, as though he had peeled away the irrelevancies to find the essence of the individual but yet universal mind. He considered himself a representative sample of one. What he discovered about himself he considered true for everyone. He was unaware that there was much about his "personal" psychology that his theories could not explain. He strove for a comprehensive theory of the human mind just as the physicists were striving similarly to explain the fundamentals of matter. Antireligious as he was, he could not see how his work reflected a faith in a view of the world derived from what he had absorbed in his education as a scientist. He understood how a child "absorbs" aspects of the family context (much more than he did how the family "absorbs" the child) but how that same absorption process occurs between individual and family, on the one hand, and features of other socially ordered contexts, on the other, was not germane to his psychology. The complexities of the individual mind were figure; the complexities of its socially ordered contexts were ground—and a very circumscribed ground. So, to take but one example, Freud strove mightily to understand women, and to the day he died he never could securely answer the question "What do women *want*?" To Freud this was neither a strange question nor an indication that he was allowing himself to be distracted from asking other questions about women. What were the role and status of women in the social order? Why did the role and status of women differ so from those of men? Why do we blithely accept such differences? One could add many more questions that Freud could have asked had he been as sensitive to how his conceptions of gender were rather directly learned by him in the course of growing up in a particular family and social order as he was to the different meanings of a circumscribed interpersonal transaction. For Freud there was a social order but it was out there, and how the out there shaped the structure and content of his being and, therefore, his theories he never saw as a central psychological issue.

In this chapter I have emphasized three points. First, what we call a psychological conception or theory is *psychologically* shaped by one's experiences and places in ordered milieus part of a larger social order. Second, the failure to recognize this point guarantees that the social impact of these theories will have intended and unintended consequences, good and harmful in varying degrees. Third, the first two points are consequences or correlates of a psychology of individuals. In the next chapter I will further illustrate the strength in psychology of the emphasis on the individual organism by examining some presidential addresses to the American Psychological Association.

CHAPTER V

A LOOK AT SOME PRESIDENTIAL ADDRESSES TO THE AMERICAN PSYCHOLOGICAL ASSOCIATION

THE FASCINATION WITH AND EMPHASIS ON the structure and functioning of the individual characterize American psychology from its earliest beginnings as an academic discipline. Today, when we think about psychology as a field, we do not identify it only with people in the university. Many people outside the university practice psychology in both its scientific and professional aspects. As I said in an earlier chapter, there is an emerging polarization between psychologists in and outside the university, those outside tending to view those inside in pejorative terms. It has long been the case that those in the university looked upon those outside as inferior psychologists, either because they had not been motivated, or lacked the capacity, to do basic research, or because they were applying psychological principles and theories sloppily, superficially, or atheoretically. Nevertheless, they were not disowned; they were seen as practical people who tried to help others (individuals, organizations) but that effort, it seemed obvious, could hardly be rated on the same level as university people's attempts to contribute to the growing store of human knowledge.

The polarization of recent decades is along different lines. Increasingly, those outside the university disown the theorists and researchers in academia: they view their work as straying more and more from the real world, and this in a traditional setting seemingly intractable to change. The response of academics has been a muted and complex one, ranging from feelings of embattlement and rejection, to quiet

despair because the high traditions of the university are being subverted by the misleaders, the misled, and the uninformed, to the formation of new groups and organizations whose memberships are
homogeneous in the values they hold about the primacy of scientific
theorizing and research, to agreement (by some) that the stance of
those outside the university is not without its merits.

It is characteristic of polarizations, especially if you are a partisan of
one or the other side, that you concentrate on the differences that
divide rather than the similarities that exist. This is not to deny that
the differences are important but rather to suggest that the unexamined similarities may be no less significant and, in the current instance, more fateful for the future. The major similarity I wish to
emphasize is the continuing concentration on a psychology of the individual: the primacy given to the individual's psychological structure
to the virtual exclusion of the social structure and institutional and
behavior settings in which he or she is embedded. Although the current malaise in psychology is a direct consequence of sea swell alterations in our society and the rest of the world, a consequence
acknowledged by those within and without the university, there is no
disposition to entertain the possibility that psychology's absorption
with the individual organism may be, and will continue to be, the
Achilles heel in psychology's failure to realize its stated goal to contribute, scientifically and otherwise, to human welfare. On the basis of
the previous chapter, it could be argued that psychology not only has
failed in certain areas but also, albeit unknowingly and with the best
intentions, has caused harm to a lot of groups in our society. Voltaire
said that history is written by the victors, which is another way of saying that the formulation of criteria of success, progress, and achievement is not independent of whose oxen have been gored.

Precisely because of its concentration on the individual, psychology
does not analyze its polarizations in social historical terms. They are
discussed in terms of competing values and theories and visions of the
future but not in terms of how a searched past may have contributed to
and still exists in the present. Psychologists have long been interested
in the personal histories of the individual, or of some feature of him or
her, but far less interested in the social and institutional history of the
enterprise of psychology. When psychologists delve into an
individual's history, it is not for the narrow purpose of describing
events and listing the dramatis personae but rather to infer (according
to some theoretical conceptions) processes, axioms, and pictures

without which the events and cast of characters have little or no meaning and with which present and past gain continuity.

The social historical context—the ground out of which the individual *and* the psychologist emerge as figure—has, for all practical
purposes, held no interest for psychology. It would be correct, though
misleading, to say that psychology never has denied the importance of
the social historical ground. It is misleading because it suggests that a
deliberate choice was made to place the emphasis on the individual. As
we have seen, such was not the case: in its separation and then divorce
from philosophy, and in its embrace of the scientific ethos and
methodology, psychology ended up with the nature and structure of
individual behavior (overt and covert) as the object of interest and
study. If psychology were to be scientific, it needed a subject matter
amenable to scientific study, preferably in a laboratory. And if
psychology were to be true to scientific tradition, experimentation had
to be possible and that meant that one sought to isolate psychological
phenomena from extraneous, contaminating influences. And in practice that meant isolating not only the individual from his or her social
historical context but also parts of the person from other parts of
himself or herself.

We cannot explain what happened merely by pointing to extant
theories or to conceptions of the scientific enterprise, because what
they reflect is an implicit world view of how the social world is organized and works, the centrality of science in that social world, and,
fatefully, the power of knowledge to have rational and desirable impacts on society. In such a world view scientific psychology would provide a grateful society with the knowledge it needed on its onward
and upward course to human betterment. That knowledge would be
about the individual mind: its contents, processes, structure, and
vicissitudes. *That* was the knowledge psychology had to obtain for and
provide to society, and psychology was humble about how long it
would take for the new science to provide such knowledge. There was
no disposition to question psychology's view of how society is organized, works, and changes. They knew that psychology was in that society but their world view did not dispose them to describe and question
that relationship. It was not seen as a problematic relationship. Society
needed a scientific psychology, of that psychologists had no doubt
whatsoever. But how did psychology need society? The answer implicit in psychology's world view was equally unambiguous: let us do

our thing and you will be the beneficiary; stay out of our way until we can tell you the way to go; the relationships between knowledge and action, between the laboratory and society, will present few or no problems because of the scientific knowledge that psychology will provide; and the values that inform the scientific endeavor and those that inform social action are consistent with each other.

Psychology wanted to be, and assumed that society would allow it to be, asocial until it could provide the basis for social action and change. This stance exposed the level of knowledge that psychology had about how society is organized, works, and shapes lives. It was also a stance in which the past, compared to the present and the future, occupied a minor position. Psychology reflected a world view of the future unclouded by anything except the conceptual difficulties inherent in rigorously developing and testing theories. How psychology would be shaped by the social factors determining who were or would become psychologists, by where psychology was housed in an institutional sense (i.e., in the university), by the political, economic, social, and demographic features of the society, and by changing alignments and power relationships on the international scene—these had no place in the world view of psychologists. Psychology was a part of the world but apart from it. No thought was given to the possibility that there might be, or had to be, some intrinsic relationships between the content, foci, and methods of psychology and the place of psychologists in the social order.

To pursue these points let us turn to a collection of presidential addresses to the American Psychological Association (Hilgard, 1978). The book is divided into four parts: the first twenty-five years (1892–1916), World War I through World War II, psychology after World War II, and the recent years. These divisions suggest the degree to which the focus and substance of psychology reflected, and still reflect, changes in the larger society, national and international. It is nearer the truth to say that these divisions suggest how psychology has been overtaken by events and ideas never given a place in its theories.

Let us start where Hilgard starts: William James's "Knowing of Things Together." The following passage is vintage James:

> You will agree with me that I have brought no new insight to the subject, and that I have only gossiped to while away this unlucky presidential

hour to which the constellations doomed me at my birth. But since gossip we have had to have, let me make the hour more gossipy still by saying a final word about the position taken up in my own *Principles of Psychology* on the general question before us, a position which, as you doubtless remember, was so vigorously attacked by our colleague from the University of Pennsylvania at our meeting in New York a year ago. That position consisted in this, that I proposed to simply eliminate from psychology "considered as a natural science" the whole business of ascertaining *how* we come to know things together or to know them at all. Such considerations, I said, should fall to metaphysics. That we do know things, sometimes singly and sometimes together, is a fact. That states of consciousness are the vehicle of the knowledge, and depend on brain states, are two other facts. And I thought that a natural science of psychology might legitimately confine itself to tracing the functional variations of these three sorts of fact, and ascertaining and tracing what determinate bodily states are the condition when the states of mind know determinate things and groups of things. Most states of mind can be designated only by naming what objects they are "thoughts-of," i.e., what things they know.

Most of those which know compound things are utterly unique and solitary mental entities demonstrably different from any collection of simpler states to which the same objects might be singly known. Treat them all as unique in entity, I said then; let their complexity reside in their plural cognitive function; and you have a psychology which, if it doesn't ultimately explain the facts, also does not, in expressing them, make them self-contradictory (as the associationist psychology does when it calls them many ideas fused into one idea) or pretend to explain them (as the soul-theory so often does) by a barren verbal principle.

My intention was a good one, and a natural science infinitely more complete than the psychologies we now possess could be written without abandoning its terms. Like all authors, I have, therefore, been surprised that this child of my genius should not be more admired by others— should, in fact, have been generally either misunderstood or despised. But do not fear that on this occasion I am either going to defend or to re-explain the bantling. I am going to make things more harmonious by simply *giving it up*. I have become convinced since publishing that book that no conventional restriction *can* keep metaphysical and so-called epistemological inquiries out of the psychology books. I see, moreover, better now than then that my proposal to designate mental states merely by their cognitive function leads to a somewhat strained way of talking of dreams and reveries, and to quite an unnatural way of talking of some emotional states. I am willing, consequently, henceforward that mental contents should be called complex, just as their objects are, and this even in psychology. Not because their parts are separable, as the parts of objects are; not because they have an eternal or quasi-eternal individual existence, like the parts of objects; for the various "contents" of which they are parts are integers, existentially, and their parts only live as long as *they* live. Still, *in* them, we can call parts, parts.—But when, without circumlocution or disguise, I thus come over to your views, I insist that those of you who applaud me (if any such there be) should recognize the obligations which the new agreement imposes on yourselves. Not till you have dropped the old phrases, so absurd or so empty, of ideas "self-compounding" or "united by a spiritual principle"; not till you have in your turn succeeded in some such long inquiry into conditions as the one I have just failed in; not till you have laid bare more of the nature of that altogether unique kind of complexity in unity which mental states involve; not till then, I say, will psychology reach any real benefit from the conciliatory spirit of which I have done what I can to set an example. (Pp. 49–51)

Without in any way suggesting that the issues James is struggling with are unimportant, I would point out that his emphasis, as it was in his deservedly influential textbook, was on the internal states of individuals. Knowing, states of consciousness, brain states, dreams, reveries, emotions—these and other features of the "stuff of experience" are what psychology has to understand in their complexity. And, he tells us, it will not be an easy task. But he leaves us in no doubt about where the emphasis in psychology should be: the psyche and its neurophysiological substrata. James, of course, assumed that the individual psyche is neither disembodied nor dissocialized, and he was an incisive critic of interpretations of experiments that confused the structure and interrelationships among external stimuli with those of the "complexity in unity" of internal states. However, James's individual was hardly social in the sense that no account was taken of the social matrices of which he was a part, of the relationships between those ordered matrices and other ordered features of the society, and of the ways by which tradition and social history give shape and direction to lives, groups, classes, and institutions. *That* substratum, that *social* "complexity in unity" was crowded out of James's formulations by his focus on the internal states of the individual. He was sensitive to and could describe beautifully the role of discrete situations in relation to an aspect of an individual's experience that interested James; the in-

dividual and the situation fuse into a unity that compels our interest
and engenders in us the sense of understanding. But situations do not
take place in a social vacuum. The way an individual describes or experiences a situation or the way an observer would describe and experience that same situation reflects the influence of near and far, past
and present societal features. The physical appearance and structure
of the situation—whether it takes place in an airplane, a church, a con-
cert hall, a classroom, a restaurant, or a laboratory—are not ordered
randomly; they may be so familiar that it never occurs to us that the
situation's physical appearance and structure have a long history in
the workings of the society. And if the situation involves more than one
person—for example, an experimenter in a laboratory with a human
subject—who would deny that the structure, direction, and basis of
their interaction reflect a good deal about our society?

The fact is that such denial was made all too easy for psychologists
because they were riveted on the individual psyche. Precisely because
James wrote about and conceptualized the individual psyche as compellingly, clarifyingly, and creatively as he did, he was like a magnet
pulling others in his direction. This is not to say that psychologists
were disposed to go in other directions but rather that James's
brilliance blinded others to alternative ways of looking at and placing
the individual. It is ironic that James, who was the opposite of
dogmatic and whose interests in the varieties of human experience
were many (indeed boundless), should have been a major influence in
psychology's adoption of a narrow focus. It is doubly ironic that the
man who articulated pragmatism so clearly and cogently, who set such
store by the relationships between mental contents and their consequences in action, and who undercut the traditional assumptions on
which the mind-body, subjective-objective, internal-external dichotomies were based should have come to be regarded as a philosopher: a
label James prized highly but one that reflects psychology's narrow
conception of its boundaries.

One of the charming aspects of James's writings is his use of his
own experiences to illustrate a point. To take but one example (James,
1971):

> Suppose me to be sitting here in my library at Cambridge, at ten
> minutes' walk from "Memorial Hall," and to be thinking truly of the lat-
> ter object. My mind may have before it only the name, or it may have a
> clear image, or it may have a very dim image of the hall, but such intrin-

sic differences in the image make no difference in its cognitive function. Certain *extrinsic* phenomena, special experiences of conjunction, are what impart to the image, be it what it may, its knowing office.

For instance, if you ask me what hall I mean by my image, and I can tell you nothing; or if I fail to point or lead you toward the Harvard Delta; or if, being led by you, I am uncertain whether the hall I see be what I had in mind or not; you would rightly deny that I had ''meant'' that particular hall at all, even though my mental image might to some *degree* have resembled it. The resemblance would count in that case as coincidental merely, for all sorts of things of a kind resemble one another in this world without being held for that reason to take cognizance of one another.

On the other hand, if I can lead you to the hall, and tell you of its history and present uses; if in its presence I feel my idea, however imperfect it may have been, to have led hither and to be now *terminated;* if the associates of the image and of the felt hall run parallel, so that each term of the one context corresponds serially, as I walk, with an answering term of the others; why then my soul was prophetic, and my idea must be, and by common consent would be, called cognizant of reality. That percept was what I *meant,* for into it my idea has passed by conjunctive experiences of sameness and fulfilled intention. Nowhere is there jar, but every later moment continues and corroborates an earlier one. (P. 31)

The point that James is making is that the significances of an idea have to be seen in relationship to and its consequences for action. But what does this example tell us that James does not comment on? He is a professor at Harvard, has an office, and lives in a house near his office. These facts applied to very, very few people in the society of his day. As we know, the fact that James was at Harvard says a good deal about James the person and Harvard the institution. Intuitively we know it says a good deal about both but if we were forced to elaborate on the intuition, we would feel overwhelmed by the task. Comparatively speaking, we would feel less overwhelmed by James the person because we can read what he wrote, what others who knew him wrote, and the accounts of his fascinating family history. But even then, we would soon be faced with the following question: can you write about James the person—can you understand the substance and focuses of his formal contributions, which gave him such special stamp and were no less a part of his person than were his dress, dreams, eating habits, etc.—without writing about American social-political-economic-religious history in general, with special emphasis on

Boston-Cambridge? What do we mean when we say of James, as we would of any individual, that he was of his time and place, other than that he bore the imprint of the larger and smaller societies? And do we not also mean that this imprinting took place to such an extent and with such efficiency that James himself could only partially, at best, comprehend?

It has been said that William James wrote like a novelist and his brother, Henry, wrote like a psychologist. The author of that assessment must mean, I assume, that the characters in Henry James's novels are always depicted in the context of a highly ordered social surround without which what we call individual lives make no sense. These are novels in which the social basis of a society is sometimes figure and sometimes ground but never absent. What makes his individual characters tick is always seen in relation to how the society ticks. Just as William James objected to the traditional formulations of the inside-outside dichotomy, Henry James, in his own way, took the same position about the individual-society separation. Henry was far more than William the observer and critic of the social scene and far more sensitive to how he himself was a creature of his society. If Henry wrote like a psychologist, he was using a very atypical psychology.

I am intrigued by the fantasy that Henry and William James were friends rather than brothers and that Henry decided to write a novel in which William is a central character. But the very concept of central character reflects the prepotent tendency to concentrate on the individual and obscures the fact that in many of Henry's novels there are two "characters" the boundaries between whom are porous: the individual, on the one hand, and a geographically located, highly ordered social stratum, on the other. We could learn a great deal about Boston, Cambridge, and Harvard from our hypothetical novel —probably far more than any psychologist could have told us— but what is so intriguing is how Henry James would have understood the relationships between the content and directions of William's formal psychology and his place in the Boston-Cambridge-Harvard social structure. Henry, I assume, would not have said that one caused the other or that they were very highly correlated but, more simply, that they were not independent of each other—an approach far different from that of psychology, as we have seen. William James' contributions to human thought and knowledge were mammoth and have stood the test of time, but that is no warrant for overlooking that these contributions had the unintended consequence of solidifying a narrowness in psychology's focus, a narrowness that has repeatedly been exposed whenever psychology ventures forth into society.

At the meeting in the year following James's address, J. McKeen Cattell gave his presidential address, "The Progress of Psychology as an Experimental Science." Very near the beginning of his address Cattell says:

> While our confidence in the future of psychology rests on a knowledge of its intrinsic vitality, we are able for the convincing of others to offer the brute argument of material success. The academic growth of psychology in America during the past few years is almost without precedent. The work begun by James at Harvard, Ladd at Yale, and Hall at Johns Hopkins not more than about fifteen years ago has become an important factor in our universities. Psychology is a required subject in the undergraduate curriculum wherever studies are required, and among university courses psychology now rivals the other leading sciences in the number of students attracted and in the amount or original work accomplished.
>
> In addition to the objective test of university recognition we may regard productiveness in publication. There are in America three journals of general science, in all of which psychology is treated as are the other sciences, and there are special journals as follows: mathematics, 3; astronomy, 3; physics, 1; chemistry, 2; geology, 2; botany, 2; zoology, 1; physiology, 0; psychology, 2. A comparison of these journals will not discredit those devoted to psychology; and it should be noted that we have in addition to these at least two journals of philosophy and two journals of education in which psychology occupies a prominent place. It would be difficult to select by an objective criterion the most important books published in America during the past ten years, but if we may regard the judgment of foreign nations as the most probable verdict of posterity, the books written by members of this Association will stand well to the front among American contributions to science.
>
> We must admit that the rapid growth of psychology in America has been due to conditions of the soil as well as to vitality of the germ. The more complete absorption of the college president by executive work has made necessary the transferring of his former prerogative of teacher of philosophy to the special student, while the development of the university with elective courses has permitted the easy introduction of a new study. (Pp. 53–54)

Cattell, like other psychologists of his day (with the possible exception of James), had no doubts about "progress." Psychology, and by implication society, was securely on the road to human betterment; growth and differentiation were obvious, proof-positive measures that all was well with psychology—aspects of an unexamined world view by no means peculiar to psychologists. Still another aspect of Cattell's world view, reflected in this and other parts of his address, is that to the extent that psychology truly becomes a science it will be part of the cause of societal transformations. Knowledge transforms not only science but also society; that is, as a social institution science is structured, operates, and follows rules and values no different from those of the larger society or any of its major divisions. Precisely because these are aspects of his world view—axioms without which what he says, proposes, and hopes makes no sense—society, for Cattell, can remain an inchoate entity awaiting the knowledge that it wishes for its transformation. While society waits, psychology will push forward scientifically into the unexplored fundamentals of individual functioning.

Take the sentence "We must admit that the rapid growth of psychology in America has been due to conditions of the soil as well as to vitality of the germ." One might expect that what would follow this sentence would be a discussion of American society and those of its features that have shaped psychology's substance, style, organization, and growth. No such discussion occurs; instead, Cattell tells us how changes in the university have facilitated psychology's growth. Why was the university changing? What did such changes suggest about changes in the society at large? Would psychology's independence in the university, altering as it must its relationships with other disciplines, have no bearing on the substance and direction of this nascent field? Is the substance of a field completely independent of its place and role in a complex, changing institution? Can the spirit of entrepreneurship, so well reflected in Cattell's life, have no influence on what one decides to sell?

Cattell's lack of sensitivity to the structural, economic, political, and cultural features of society can best be judged by comparing his outlook to that of Veblen (1957), who, a decade after Cattell's address, wrote his classic *The Higher Education in America,* written in 1905 but not published for some years after. Veblen was not in an academic sense a psychologist—the social sciences were never comfortable with him, and he resisted pigeonholing—and he has had no impact on psychology. But he was one of the few who saw clearly that an individual psychology has to be a social psychology, and by social he meant the structure of, the interrelationships and conflicts among, groups, classes, and institutions, which react differently to a common ideology (itself a derivative of an implicit world view) grounded in a distinctive history. Who you are, where you are, where you see yourself going, and how you see others, i.e., your "psychology"—the *starting* point for understanding these questions is the highly ordered, differentiated social fabric. That is what Veblen would have meant by "soil" and he would have had all kinds of doubts and forebodings about the "vitality of the germ." For Veblen, the substance, defined boundaries, and directions of psychology were as much grounded in the social soil as in the peculiarities and creativity of individual psychologists.

Let us look at another paragraph in Cattell's address:

> We may be glad that experimental psychology has practical applications in spite of quasi-official dicta to the contrary. In the United States more than one hundred and fifty million dollars, collected by enforced taxation, is spent annually on public schools in the attempt to "change human natures." President Eliot [of Harvard] says that nothing is accomplished in these schools except the training of the memory, and his colleague, our retiring president, tells us that the memory cannot be trained. Surely in education, which extends from birth to death, we can learn by experiments on these senses and the mind what may be done to fit the individual to his environment. It should not be forgotten that we not only hold the clay in our hands to mold for honor or dishonor, but we also have the ultimate decision as to what material we shall use. The physicist can turn his pig iron into steel, and so can we ours; but he cannot alter the quantities of gold and iron in his world, whereas we can in ours. Our responsibility is, indeed, very great. By one psychological experiment we injure the eyesight of our children in the schools, and by another psychological experiment we discover the defect and fit glasses to correct it. It seems to me certain that experimental psychology has widereaching practical applications, not only in education, but also in medicine, in the fine arts, in political economy, and, indeed, in the whole conduct of life. (Pp. 61)

Cattell was well aware that psychology was allergic to practical applications. Although Cattell can be described as one of the most (if not the most) creative entrepreneurs in the history of psychology, I think that what he says in this paragraph represents well the ultimate hope of all psychologists, i.e., to transform society. What is so noteworthy in the paragraph for my purposes is Cattell's assurance that we understand the culture of schools, how and why it works as it does, and how it shapes the thinking and actions of those in it. The pupil (the clay) is what interests Cattell—"what may be done to fit the individual to his environment." What is the environment? Why is nothing "accomplished in these schools except the training of memory"? Why should the findings of psychological experiments transfer readily into school practices? Why should we aim "to fit the individual to his environment"? For Cattell the individual is figure and school-society is an undifferentiated background. The basic problem for Cattell is arriving at laws about the individual mind. The practical problems in application are engineering in nature. The belief in the basic-applied, theory-practice dichotomy was on one side of psychology's coin; on the other side was the individual-society dichotomy. That these were fake dichotomies, or that there were other ways of viewing the world that made these dichtomies unnecessary, were possibilities unthinkable to psychologists, given their picture of how the world was organized and worked.

Let us listen again to Cattell:

> Psychology has long been and properly remains the gateway to architectonic philosophy. It may be that experiment cannot answer the final questions of philosophy, but the world-view of each of us depends increasingly on what the natural and exact sciences contribute to it. The white light of philosophy can only result from the proper commingling of the colors of the sciences. Systems of philosophy, elaborated prior to the development of modern science or without regard to this, may receive our admiration as poetry, but they cannot claim our adherence as truth. To allot to science those subjects concerning which we have knowledge, and to reserve for philosophy those questions concerning which we know nothing, is evidently subversive of philosophy. Epistemology, ethics, logic and aesthetics are regarded as philosophic disciplines, but they rest increasingly on psychology. Epistemology depends on the psychology of perception and may be nothing else. Works on ethics, logic and aesthetics take increasing account of psychological facts; indeed, as our knowledge increases, the distinction between a normative and a descriptive science becomes somewhat tenuous. The twilight of philosophy can be changed to its dawn only by the light of science, and psychology can contribute more light than any other science (Pp. 63–64)

Nothing could be further from Cattell's thoughts than the possibility that psychology's world view was and would be more a creature of society than it would be of science; that in the coming decades psychology would be transformed less by the exactitudes of science than by changes in the larger society and world. Psychology did not have a Janus-like stance. It faced in only one direction:

> A comparison of modern text-books of psychology, such as those by James, Ladd, Baldwin, and Dewey, with older works bears irrefutable witness to the introduction of the results of physiological and psychological experiment. I shall undertake the *argumentum ad hominem* in the case of James, who said at our last meeting that "curious phenomena of the dissociation of consciousness . . . throw more new light on human nature than the work of all psycho-physical laboratories put together." On taking down James' *Psychology*—which has breathed the breath of life into the dust of psychology—and turning at random to the even hundred pages, I find that the first is entirely taken up with the measurement of the temperature of the brain in relation to thought; the second is on continuity of consciousness with time measurements; the third a description of the bodily movements giving the consciousness of self; the fourth on the relation of the two hemispheres of the brain and of bodily movements to self-consciousness; the fifth on the relative intensity of sensations and images; the sixth on the association of ideas; the seventh on observations and experiments on the mistaken interpretation of sense-stimuli; the eighth on the relation of movements of the eyes to the perception of space; the ninth on the factors distinguishing the perception of reality; the tenth on instinctive actions; the eleventh on muscular sensations; the twelfth on hypnotic suggestion. These topics illustrate very fairly the field covered by modern psychology. They nearly all rest upon psychophysical observations and experiments, and in cases where observations predominate it is evident that they will soon be superseded by actual experiments from our laboratories yielding quantitative results. (Pp. 61–62)

There could not be a clearer statement about psychology's emphasis on the individual psyche. In quoting James against James, Cattell leaves no doubt that the individual psyche is what psychology must concentrate on. To his eternal credit James never wavered in his belief that one seeks knowledge and understanding wherever one can find them and that to rate laboratory findings above all other methodologies and sites is ridiculous. James did breathe life into the dust of psychology, which is why he became increasingly appalled at psychology's restricted focus. Cattell's respectful criticism of James may have been the beginning of the process whereby James was redefined by psychology from psychologist to philosopher.

With one striking exception, which I shall discuss in chapter 6, the next four presidential addresses in the Hilgard book continue the emphasis on the individual organism, and there is no point in discussing them, however significant they are for other purposes. The titles of the addresses convey the flavor of the emphasis:

1. James Rowland Angell, "The Province of Functional Psychology."
2. E. L. Thorndike, "Ideo-Motor Action."
3. R. S. Woodworth, "A Revision of Imageless Thought."
4. J. B. Watson, "The Place of the Conditioned Reflex in Psychology."

We then come to Yerkes's address, "Psychology in Relation to the War." Yerkes uses the occasion to "outline the history of the organizing of psychological military service. I shall limit myself strictly to the activities of the present year, 1917." This address is very significant for my purposes because it was the first time that psychology in its organized form (the American Psychological Association) sought energetically to become immersed in social policy and action. As Yerkes puts it:

> In this country, for the first time in the history of our science, a general organization in the interests of certain ideal and practical aims has been effected. Today, American psychology is placing a highly trained and eager personnel at the service of military organizations. We are acting not individually but collectively on the basis of common training and common faith in the practical value of our work. At the first call American psychologists responded promptly and heartily, therefore the length to which the development of our work has progressed and the measure of service which has been attained. (Pp. 189)

To shed light on the contents of Yerkes's address, as well as to give the reader some basis for comprehending the questions I shall raise, the following excerpts will suffice:

MINUTES OF SPECIAL MEETING OF THE COUNCIL OF THE
AMERICAN PSYCHOLOGICAL ASSOCIATION

The president reported his investigations concerning the possibility of the cooperation of psychologists in a scientific capacity in the present emergency. He described his trip to Ottawa, Toronto, and Montreal, where he found the authorities very much interested in the possibility of psychological assistance. His impression was that they realized that they had made a mistake in not using psychological methods for the selection of recruits and for reeducation from the beginning of the war. The president later went to Washington to consult with the National Research Council.

It was voted that the president be instructed to appoint committees from the membership of the American Psychological Association to render to the government of the United States all possible assistance with psychological problems arising from the present military emergency.

PLAN FOR THE PSYCHOLOGICAL EXAMINING OF RECRUITS TO ELIMINATE THE MENTALLY UNFIT

Whereas the Council of the American Psychological Association is convinced that in the present emergency American psychologists can substantially serve the government under the medical corps of the Army and Navy by examining recruits with respect especially to intellectual deficiency, psychopathic tendencies, nervous instability, and inadequate self-control, it has voted to present to the proper military authorities the following plan and suggestions for psychological service.

This is not intended as a reflection on the work of the military medical examiner, but instead as an offer of special professional aid in a time of unusual strain, pressure and haste. Psychologically incompetent recruits are peculiarly dangerous risks with respect to disaster in action, incapacity, and subsequent pension claims. For this reason and because few medical examiners are trained in the use of modern methods of psychological examining, our profession should be of extreme value to the medical corps.

It is proposed: . . .

(a) In consultation with medical officers and company officers the psychologist should prepare a list of all men in a given company for whom special psychological examination is indicated by exceptional or unsatisfactory behavior.

(b) With this special list before him the psychological examiner should summon the men of the company to appear, one at a time, in his examining room. Each should there be subjected to a short series of mental measurements, the necessary time for which should not exceed ten minutes. The result of these measurements should be a rough estimate of the mental status and chief characteristics of the individual and consequent classification as mentally *inferior, normal* or *superior.* Special attention should be given to men whose mental fitness had been questioned by medical or other officers.

(c) The normal group (probably 80 to 90 per cent of all) should be passed, without further examination, as mentally competent. The inferiors should be eliminated from the service. The superiors, time permitting, should be systematically examined for indications of their special value in the military organization.

(d) The special examination for inferiors (or superiors) would require from thirty to sixty minutes. It should consist of measurements of various forms and aspects of response, among which should appear motor characteristics (for example, quickness, steadiness, and fatigability), observation, memory, suggestibility, adaptability or rapidity of learning, judgment, reasoning power, instinctive and emotional traits.

(e) The psychological staff should discuss the examination record of each inferior man and vote on the question of recommending to the medical officer his rejection or discharge from the service. (Pp. 194–198)

How shall we understand the behavior of psychologists (individually and collectively) in relation to the war effort? More specifically, how do psychological theories, past and present, help us understand the dramatic changes that took place in the lives of psychologists? After all, psychologists are people and their theories about human behavior are no less applicable to themselves than to other people. Does anyone doubt that the single most important fact with which one would start is that *their* country was at war? What does it mean when a person says "my" or "our" country? Why the possessive adjective? The answer, in brief, is that it took a special circumstance, like a war, for psychologists to recognize how much their way of life—their thinking, values, behavior, international perspective, we-they dichotomies—was grounded in a particular society. They were in that society, and that society was in them, just as the oxygen in and outside of them was part of their living system. They knew they were not Germans, or French, or British, or Russian. They were *Americans*. When the United States entered World War I it seemed natural and proper for psychologists to rally round the flag. It required little or no thinking. And that is the point: in formulating their theories, practices, values, and goals psychologists never thought how these formulations may have directly reflected *their* society. They knew they lived in their society—they were *Americans* *—and to a degree knew what that meant in a personal sense, but the possibil-

*They did not comprehend that Canadians, Mexicans, and Peruvians, for instance, also consider themselves Americans, but very different kinds of Americans living in very different social soils.

ity that embeddedness was a powerful factor in the shape, substance, and direction of their psychologizing was never considered. They wanted a psychology independent both of themselves and of society. That this may have been an impossibility, an illusion, never occurred to them; the shape and content of psychology had to have a life of its own. It was a very unselfconscious, asocial psychology. It was not a psychology that could explain psychologists.

Few things are as diagnostic of the unverbalized world view as the reactions of people before, during, and after a war, if only because war requires people to answer certain questions: what kind of world do we live in, why do wars occur, how do we justify killing others and sacrificing our countrymen and possibly ourselves, why are we the good guys and they the bad guys? War arouses pictures of ourselves, our allies, our enemies, pictures containing concrete images of individuals who think and feel in different ways and who are arrayed for and against each other. They are pictures painted with passion and commitment, sure signs that the social soil on which one stands is threatened and needs protection—and will remain unexamined unless on a purely conceptual or theoretical level there is something to warn you about dangers in how you are thinking and acting. No such warnings existed for psychologists. For such warnings to have existed, there would have to have been a psychology that recognized that society is as much inside as outside people and that it is a fiction to regard the substance and style of psychology as independent of the society.

If the onset of World War I demonstrated to psychologists the obvious significance of being citizens of the United States, it also forced on them the implications of the fact that this was a country of immigrants from many different lands. If psychologists unreflectively accepted the implications of *their* embeddedness in the society, they were equally unreflective about what it meant to be an immigrant in this country, i.e., to be of two countries. What needs to be noted, and is not contained in Yerkes's address, is that there had long been raging controversies in this country, in which psychologists participated, about what the waves of immigrants were doing to the social fabric. Here again the psychology of the time had no way of formulating the issue except in terms of genetics and variations in tested intelligence. Intelligence (like genes) was *in* the individual, and if on average the individuals in one immigrant group tested lower than those from another group, it said a good deal about the differences in their gene pools.

The major problem facing psychologists in World War I was how to weed out mental incompetents. For psychologists mental incompetence was not a stigma but a brute individual fact the consequences of which for the society (the native stock and establishment, that is) took precedence over anything else.

It is interesting how in his address Yerkes emphasizes psychology's role in the war as a scientific one, glossing over the obvious fact that psychology had put itself in the business of serving the society as it saw it and wanted it to be. One could not read an address more laden with values, with the outcroppings of an unexamined world view, with the consequences of the fiction that psychologists' theories of the human psyche do not reflect the psychologist's socialization.

I am *not* advancing the argument that psychologists were prejudiced and that their theories were in the service of these prejudices. To advance that argument would be, for my purposes, a distraction from what I consider an issue that determines the strength, duration, and consequences of prejudice: can the substance, style, and direction of a psychological theory that purports to explain human behavior be independent of the ways in which and degree to which the theorist's society is in him or her? Can a psychological theory be valid that does not explicitly deal with the fusion of (not the dichotomy between) individual and society? Can a psychology that avoids dealing with that fusion avoid failure in social action and lessen the chances that such action will come to be seen as harmful?

On the very day these words were written there appeared a full-page advertisement by a mass media magazine, *Psychology Today,* in the *New York Times* (August 28, 1979). Here is part of the advertisement:

I.Q. CHAOS

In the chaos of controversy, the standard I.Q. exam is flunking the test.

Many educational psychologists feel that I.Q. testers have failed to answer two all-important questions.

What is intelligence? What have I.Q. tests actually measured?

The National Education Association, with a membership of almost 2 million teachers, has called for the abolition of standardized intelligence tests because they are "at best wasteful, and at worst, destructive."

California and the cities of New York and Washington, D.C. have in fact banned these tests in public schools.

The September issue of *Psychology Today* explores "The New Generation of Intelligence Tests" that could put an end to the chaos.

Yale psychologist Robert Sternberg says in *P.T.* that psychologists know "almost nothing about what it is that they have been measuring. The tests have proved overall to have only low to moderate power to predict such things as future job performance, income and status, or overall happiness and adjustment."

But Sternberg feels we have new insights into defining intelligence. He doubts that intelligence is a single factor, but rather a collection of abilities, some of which have been ignored on standard I.Q. tests.

And Senior Editor Berkeley Rice investigates a variety of new ways to measure mental ability. Tests that measure the intelligence of preverbal infants by using toy cars and dolls. Tests that stimulate the electrical circuitry of the brain and map the results with computers. Tests showing the influence of TV-watching on how we process information. Tests that measure the "components" of intelligence.

The security with which Yerkes and others pursued their science is hardly in evidence, washed away by rivers of criticism originating in the awareness that psychological theories and tests, developed without sensitivity to the nature of our society and of the individual-society fusion, have caused lasting harm to millions of people (Sarason and Doris, 1969; Sarason and Doris, 1979). Yerkes and his colleagues never intended to cause harm. They were also aware that there was much they needed to learn, by which they meant the genetics, components, and measurement of individual intelligence. What they did not realize was that the concept of intelligence is a social invention, inevitably reflecting social time and place, not a "thing" in an individual. Without this realization the conditions for causing harm remain, just as today, when we are told that intelligence consists of many factors. The original invention was too simple, just as the early conceptions of the atom grossly oversimplified its fantastically complex structure. The search goes on! The more things change, the more they remain the same. Given psychology's emphasis, together with its basically asocial stance, it could hardly be otherwise.

Another feature of Yerkes's address requires comment. It is a more subtle feature, which Yerkes handles with much tact. It concerns how and where to put psychologists in the armed services. Yerkes was a major in the Sanitary Corps! Only medical personnel could be in the Medical Corps. Indeed, many psychologists could be employed only in civilian status. Psychologists were faced with a variant of what has been called the port of entry problem: how do you enter and become part of an organization to which you want to be helpful but which views you as a stranger? (In this respect psychologists were like immigrants, but that similarity went unnoticed.) Psychologists viewed the problem as a tactical one that required interpersonal skills and political-organizational pressures. It was seen as an applied problem, an engineering one, a political one in the broad sense. But what psychological theories or findings could be used to deal with the port of entry issue?

There was nothing in psychological theory or findings to use. What psychologists did employ were largely personal, implicit "theories" about the nature of our society in general, how it works, and how one gets things done in it. If these theories were implicit, it was in part because the purposes they served were not considered central or even important to psychology. And those purposes were to understand how society is organized and how people's places in it determine their thinking and actions. It is irrelevant what the substance of these theories were and the degree to which they had validity. The important point is that these theories were informal and implicit even though they concerned the structured individual–structured society relationship. In a formal sense, however, the psychologist focused on one part of the relationship, and in adopting that restricted focus he avoided an issue that in his "informal" life he had unreflectively dealt with and resolved, thus making it all to easy to regard the port of entry problem as an applied one. Then, as now, psychology's efforts to immerse itself in and to influence society produced, in my view, one very clear-cut finding: psychological theory has been a massive hindrance to psychologists' comprehension of the society that is in them and in those people they seek to help or influence.

The presidential addresses reprinted by Hilgard are diverse in many respects and they are of more than historical interest. For the most part, they deal with issues that were and are both interesting and important. The quality of these addresses is not at issue. What is at issue are the significances of the overwhelming emphasis on the individual organism. If I regard this emphasis as egregiously unfortunate for psychology, it is because of two facts. The first is that psychologists, individually and collectively, see and proclaim their work as contributing to the public welfare; society will—either now or in the future—be better off by virtue of having assimilated into its structure and functions the findings of psychologists. Even when psychologists, like others in the scientific or scholarly community, talk about knowledge for knowledge's sake, they are not asking society to indulge their need for personal or intellectual pleasure or to accord them a freedom that has no boundaries or societal obligations. The philologist who studies Hittite dialects, the scholar who seeks to reinterpret Shakespeare's sonnets, the biologist, comparative psychologist, or geneticist who seeks the origins and neurophysiological bases of aggressive behavior in nonhuman animals, the developmental psychologist who studies neonatal response to visual and auditory stimuli, the astronomer who spends years collecting data on a particular galaxy, and the psychologist intrigued with the nature of artificial intelligence in comparison to human intelligence—each of these people regards his or her efforts as important to society. Some hope that the society will find their work of social utility. Others assert that what society does with their work is of no concern to them and that their main purpose is to illuminate a problem that interests them and with which others are also caught up: why, then, should society support their work, indulge such personal pursuits? Their unambiguous answer would be that the society they know, the society they respect and deem worthy of protection, would be a "poorer" society if it did not support them in their pursuits, if it measured achievement only by practical results for the larger society.

From its beginnings in the modern era psychology has seen itself in relation to its contributions to society. There was never any doubt that psychology should and would, over time, impact on society. Indeed, as a newly organized discipline seeking acceptance and support from both the scientific community and the larger society, psychology promised a great deal. But it was far more knowledgeable about and interested in the scientific endeavor—its traditions, morality, culture, and achievements. As a result, the focus it adopted, the methodologies it employed, the very sites in which work was conducted (the isolated laboratory) had the effect of pushing society far down on psychology's agenda. What was unfortunate was that psychology could not be consistent with its own stated purposes. It became (and remains) an asocial psychology, removed from the social matrix to which it purports to be relevant and unable even to ask: how are the substance and directions of psychological theory related to society and the psychologist's place in it? In the cloud chamber of society how does one track

and understand psychology's path? Can the strictest adherence to
scientific objectivity eliminate all vestiges of the world view that one
inevitably and unreflectively absorbs by virtue of belonging to a particular society? Can a psychologist who seeks to conceptualize the interactions among structure, process, and content of individual
behavior, and who carefully structures or describes the context in
which that behavior will be observed, ignore the fact that both the individual and the psychologist have lived in and absorbed features of a
structured society in which their places were not randomly determined?

The second basis on which I regard psychology's emphasis to be
unfortunate is a direct consequence of the first. When I look back over
psychology's eager movement into public service—in relation to war,
public education, social reform, health policy—several impressions are
outstanding. The first is how many psychologists came quickly to feel
unprepared to understand and to deal with the intraorganizational and
interorganizational culture of the public arena. They were astounded
that truth, reason, skill, and expertise were insufficient (frequently
hindrances) to establish one's credentials or to win respect and a voice
in policy matters. They were always interacting with other individuals
whom they could see, touch, and talk to, with the result that they explained their experience and the behavior of others in individual,
motivational, or narrowly interpersonal terms: the hallmarks of an individual psychology. Because of this orientation they were not prepared for the fact that you cannot *see* the structure of an agency, you
cannot *see* a role, you cannot *see* tradition and history, you cannot *see*
values, you cannot *see* agency boundaries, you cannot *see* the agency
culture, you cannot *see* interconnections among agencies, and you cannot *see* the society in which the agencies are embedded and to which
they are responsible. Structure, role, tradition, history, values, boundaries, culture, interconnections, society—we do not see these the way
we see a pencil, a stone, or a person. We invent these concepts—role,
value, etc.—in order to make sense of questions that arise from what
we see and concretely experience. These terms are testimony to the
recognition that actions deriving from what we see frequently are inadequate or self-defeating. They are invented by necessity, the necessity for our actions to be more consistent with our purposes. Introver-
sion, self, attitude, superego, response potential, reinforcement,
conditioning, decisionmaking, projection—just as these concepts were

invented to help gain more understanding of individual behavior, resorting to abstraction in order to *re*-view and *re*-organize previous question-raising perceptions, so we have needed to invent concepts to understand and deal better with the ways in which we see ourselves and others affected by our places in society. However obvious all this may be, it has never really been taken seriously in psychology and in large measure accounts for the shocks psychologists experience when they venture forth into the real world. The frequency with which the term "real world" is used in conversation and the connotations of the term are very instructive because they tell us that there are two worlds: the real and the unreal. The former they do not understand, or if they think they understand, they do not like it, but in any event it is a complex, uncontrollable world that swamps individuality and destroys integrity. The latter, the unreal world, is never labeled as such; it is seen as an oasis, a refuge, a very different kind of world.

If psychologists have experienced shock when they have become involved in the real world, when they have seized opportunities to use their knowledge and theories to influence policies and programs, it has had little effect on their basic orientation. The resolution of cognitive dissonance, a concept and body of research quintessentially illustrative of an individual psychology, may help explain the tenacity with which psychologists hold onto their theories in the face of their obvious inadequacy as a basis for social action. But that explanation would be at best superficial because it formulates the problem as one in individuals or between individuals who are disembodied from a social historical context that is part of their psychological fabric. One must marvel at the energy psychologists devote to a Talmudic-Thomistic analysis of the structure of attitudes and the processes of attitude change, and there is no doubt they have illuminated aspects of the problem. But what they have failed to confront is the possibility that such an orientation, along with the voluminous research on which it is based, is inappropriate (if not lethal) as a basis for action in the social arena. Disappointed, disillusioned, or bloodied in their social forays, they end up keeping their orientation intact and blaming the real world for its unresponsiveness and intractability. They feel victimized but in this case they do not blame the victim.

What happened to psychologists in the arena of social action was certainly not peculiar to them. If psychology had been less individually oriented and more conscious of itself as a social institution in a particular society, it might have lessened the shocks that came as psychology willingly forged new relationships with the larger society. That, however, is less significant than the likely possibility that as a field psychology has learned little from its worldly experiences.

It is instructive to turn to a moment in history when the workings of impractical science led to a most practical product, one that our scientists and society desperately wanted. It was a moment that simultaneously illustrated the fruitfulness of scientific problem-solving and exposed its inappropriateness for solving social problems. I refer, of course, to the successful solution of all the problems, theoretical and technical, leading to the harnessing of atomic energy for military purposes. As soon as it became evident that a successful atom bomb was in the offing, some scientists began to ask themselves questions: to use it, how to use it, and how the seemingly endless uses of atomic energy for human welfare could be exploited. They saw many problems, and the substance of the problems was by no means obvious. The end result of a successful solution seemed clear: a world in which the destructive uses of atomic energy were rendered impossible or nearly so and applications for human welfare were maximized. But how do you go from here to there? What was the bearing of the scientific tradition on this problem?

As best as I can determine, none of the scientists thought they were dealing with a scientific problem. They recognized they had been catapulted into a social world that was fantastically complicated, constantly changing, and seemingly uncontrollable. It was not even a maze because that image conjures up entry points, stable pathways, and some kind of end point. The social world is not a maze. It is not even a cloud chamber because that is a device rationally constructed to record and measure predictable events. It may be a world of facts and events but it is ruled by passions. It is ironic in the extreme that at the same time that the world saw these scientists as at the apogee of human achievement, they saw themselves as angry, bewildered, impotent people. They became like most other people: passionate, committed, partisan, rhetorical, and irrational. These are not characteristics foreign to scientific controversy and investigation, but the morality of science and the critical eyes of the scientific community are effective controls against the undue influence of these characteristics. If you suspect a fellow scientist of lying and cheating or of just being a damn fool, you have ways of finding out and of spreading the word. But that means there is consensus about the rules of the game. The social world is not the scientific world. As a physicist friend once said to me: "What the hell kind of world is it?" He used exactly the same tone of petulance-anger that Professor Henry Higgins uses in *My Fair Lady* when he asks why can't women be like men? My friend went on to say: "I can't deal with a world where everybody has his own definition of the problem, facts are an intrusive annoyance and of tertiary importance, where who you are is more important than what you know, and where the need to act is more decisive than feeling secure about what the consequences will be." And he concluded: "I will stick to my world, where there are answers, and if I don't find them someone else will." When the atomic scientists entered the world of social action, that world could not be molded to fit their problem-solving strategies.

But, many social scientists thought, those were atomic scientists and one should not be surprised that when they left the world of minute matter and entered the world of human matters they faltered. After all, they were not social scientists, whose stock-in-trade is the human domain. The fact is that up until World War II the social sciences had contributed to our understanding of the social world, but with one noteworthy exception these contributions were descriptive or analytic or historical. They were not contributions stemming from the social scientist's effort to participate in and solve social problems. Like the natural scientist, the social scientist was the dispassionate observer, and deliberately so, who sought to formulate clear questions to which clear answers could be obtained. He saw his task as understanding the social world, not changing it. The one exception was economics, which for decades had an intimate tie with the practical world of government, business, industry, and finance. Early on, economists not only described the world as they saw it but also drew conclusions about what should or should not be done. They were listened to, and they took responsible positions in the social arena. Heilbronner (1961) has aptly called them the "worldly philosophers." They lived, so to speak, in two worlds: the scientific problem-solving world and the world of social action.

It was the Great Depression that really made the world of social action accessible to increasing numbers of economists. The underlying assumption, of course, was that economists had knowledge and skills that could inform public policy and action. If during the thirties the atomic scientists had developed firm friendships with their university colleagues in economics (unlikely events in the community of scholars), they would have learned much earlier than they did that scientific knowledge as power in the social arena is of a different order from that in the research community; that in the social arena one is always dealing with competing statements of a problem and there is no time or intention to experiment in implementation with one or another formulation; that the choice of formulation has less to do with data then with the traditions, values, world outlook, and spirit of the times; that the goal of social action is not to produce once-and-for-all solutions in the scientific sense but to stir the waters of change, hoping and sometimes praying that more good than harm will follow; and that the very process of formulating a problem, setting goals, and starting to act begins to change not only *your* perception of problems, goals, and actions but also, no less fateful, the perceptions of *others* related to or affected by the process in some way. *In the phenomenology of social action, problem changing rather than problem-solving is figure, and you know what that does to solutions regardless of how you define them!*

World War II opened up many opportunities for social scientists to be in social action or policy related roles. That war brought us into contact with scores of different cultures and peoples. So, as never before, anthropologists became socially important people. And sociologists and psychologists were in short supply. World War II forever changed the social sciences. They were exposed to new problems, and much that they thought they knew was proved either irrelevant or wrong. More important, they tasted the heady wine of influence and action and liked it. Government needs us, they said, and government seemed to agree. At least one noted psychologist (Doob, 1947) had his doubts and his brief paper beautifully describes the naive scientist in the world of social action. Doob's paper is noteworthy in two other respects. First, he recognized that in social action the scientist *qua* scientist is like a fish out of water: dead.

> Where social science data are inadequate or where social science itself can provide only principles or a way of approach to a problem, the social scientist must hurl himself into the debate, participate on an equal or unequal footing with men and women who are not social scientists, toss some of his scientific scruples to the winds, and fight for what seems to

him to be valid or even good. A strict adherence to the scientific *credo* in such circumstances leaves the social scientist impotent and sterile as far as policy is concerned.

Second, Doob early on learned that if he responded seriously to his and others' need for mutuality and community, even if some of those others were opponents, social action could be rewarding despite the fact that one never knows whether one is having an intended programmatic effect, i.e., that one is solving a problem.

In the aftermath of World War II the government became both patron and employer of social science. After all, the argument ran, if the government respected and supported social science research, as it did research in the biological and natural sciences, the social atom might be split and its energies harnessed for the greatest good of the greatest number. For twenty years after World War II the social sciences became, and with a vengeance, vigorous, quantitative, theoretical, and entrepreneurial. If you wanted to solve in a basic and once-and-for-all way the puzzles of individual and social behavior, you needed resources of the wall-to-wall variety. True, it would take time to learn to ask the right questions, to develop the appropriate methodologies, before you came up with the right answers. What we are after are those bedrock laws of social behavior and process that will allow a society "really" rationally to diagnose and solve its problems. Give us time (and money) and you will not regret it. In the meantime if you think we can be helpful to you with your current problems, please call on us. And call they did, and go they went. The results have been discouraging and shattering, discouraging because of the lack of intended outcomes and shattering because they have called into question the apropriateness of the scientific-rational model of problem definition and solution in social action. The concern that Nelson (1977) expresses about the social sciences generally is precisely the concern I have about psychology.

In an earlier chapter I quoted at some length from Nelson's *Moon and the Ghetto*. At the end of the quotation is the sentence "Failure to recognize the limitations of one's own perspective had made analysis of problems that require an integration of various perspectives very difficult." I would add that by perspective I mean not only explicit theories, ideas, and values but also the implicit, unverbalized world view to which what we ordinarily mean by perspective is related. That is to say, it is a problem not only of theory and data but also of un-covering and challenging as much of one's world view as possible, and at best one can do that to a partial extent. And even to do that partially requires feats of courage and imagination because what is involved is how to transcend one's own time and place. And with that statement we turn to a presidential address to the American Psychological Association in 1899, an address as atypical in thrust for psychology as it was prophetic for what happened to psychology six decades later.

CHAPTER VI

JOHN DEWEY: PROPHET WITHOUT HONOR IN PSYCHOLOGY

When John Dewey gave his American Psychological Association presidential address in 1899 in New Haven he was forty years old and a recognized, appreciated figure in the emerging field of psychology. Three years earlier he had started the Laboratory School at the University of Chicago, an important background fact for understanding his presidential address. Indeed, the Laboratory School—a setting designed as much for Dewey's intellectual needs and interests as for those of children—helped shape all of Dewey's subsequent thinking. That venture was an action in the real world, bringing him into relation with the wider Chicago community. It also generated what became a lifelong interest in connections between theory and practice, between ends and means, and between individual and society. In those days an amazing number of Chicago's very distinguished faculty, especially in sociology, were deeply involved in the community for the purpose of either research or social reform or both. It is relevant that Dewey (like others at the university) was involved in Jane Addams's Hull House, but Dewey's role as a socially conscious and critical observer of the social scene should not obscure the centrality of the theory-practice relationship to his thinking.

As we shall see, Dewey's presidential address, which in substance and direction is unique, contained the kernels of most of Dewey's later contributions. And one cannot read his address without fantasizing about what psychology might have become had it taken Dewey seriously—more correctly, had it grasped the implications of his thinking. But even today that understanding is lacking. Let us start with Dewey's introductory statement:

> In coming before you I had hoped to deal with the problem of the relationship of psychology to the social sciences and through them to social practice, to life itself. Naturally, in anticipation, I had conceived a systematic exposition of fundamental principles covering the whole ground, and giving every factor its due rating and position. That discussion is not ready to-day. I am loath, however, completely to withdraw from the subject, especially as there happens to be a certain phase of it with which I have been more or less practically occupied within the last few years. I have in mind the relation of Psychology to Education. Since education is primarily a social affair, and since educational science is first of all a social science, we have here a section of the whole field. In some respects there may be an advantage in approaching the more comprehensive question through the medium of one of its special cases. The absence of elaborated and coherent view may be made up for by a background of experience, which shall check the projective power of reflective abstraction, and secure a translation of large words and ideas into specific images. This special territory, moreover, may be such as to afford both sign-posts and broad avenues to the larger sphere, the place of psychology among the social sciences. Because I anticipate such an outcome, and because I shall make a survey of the broad field from the special standpoint taken, I make no apology for presenting this discussion to an Association of Psychologists rather than to a gathering of educators. (P. 65-66)

In his very first sentence Dewey says that there is a "problem of the relationship of psychology to the social sciences and through them to social practice, to life itself." Dewey never used words loosely and so when he says "problem" he is alerting us not to some future issue but to one in the here and now. Knowing as we do the thrust of his later writings, we see in this first sentence Dewey's recognition that the theory-practice dichotomy could not be avoided. Unlike the psychologists of his era who essentially postponed the issue, reserving it for the future when psychology would have worked out the scientific basis for social practice, Dewey is suggesting that such a position is untenable. And his admission that he is unprepared to deal with the relation of psychology and the social sciences bespeaks not only of his candor but also, and implicitly, of his recognition that the theory-practice issue was not peculiar to psychology.

What are we to make of his assertion that "educational science is first of all a social science"? Knowing Dewey's style of analysis, we are safe in saying that the assertion is an example of his skepticism about the ways we use labels to indicate differences, to obscure communalities, and adversely to affect actions. For Dewey, the field of education (its theories and practices) concerned far more than pupils, teachers, curricula, schools, etc. Educational science, precisely because schools were a creation and responsibility of society, had to bring together in a creative and productive way the contributions and points of view of all the social sciences. This was not a matter of addition or of wisely selecting this or that piece of knowledge or theory but rather of reaching for formulations that would illuminate the nature of the relationships between the educational process, setting, and participants, on the one hand, and the nature and purposes of society, on the other hand. Educational science was not about only what goes on inside a school. It was about how the "inside" exists in the "outside" and vice versa. What did the *other* social sciences have to contribute to such formulations? How would such formulations relate to existing educational practices and to changes in educational practices? Dewey says there is an absence of an "elaborated and coherent view" but that we are not without "a background of experience." That is to say, each of us has experience with the problem and, in fact, the problem arises from our experiences and not from idle musings or theory. And so when Dewey says that this background of experience shall "check the projective power of reflective abstraction, and secure a translation of large words and ideas into specific images," he is telling us again to beware of the pitfalls of the usual theory-practice dichotomy. The need for theory arises from a problem we have experienced in a context, and that theory must lead us directly back to that experience and context in clarifying ways and not become an end in itself or a formulation irrelevant to the problem that gave rise to it. To "secure a translation of large words and ideas into specific images"—theory and practice, the abstract and the concrete, are for Dewey arbitrary ways of describing an integral process.

"I make no apology for presenting this discussion to an Association of Psychologists rather than to a gathering of educators." This forthright statement suggests that the problem he was raising was a fundamental one to which psychology could not be indifferent and that the directions psychology was taking would be ultimately self-defeating. These influences come out more explicitly later in the address.

Dewey then notes that school practice has a definite psychological basis: "teachers are already possessed by specific psychological assumptions which control their theory and practice". In this very simple statement Dewey recognizes that behind theory and practice (and their relations) are assumptions akin to what I have called the axioms and pictures of the unverbalized world view. He articulates two of these assumptions without which the theories and practices of teachers would make no sense:

> One is the assumption of fundamental distinction between child psychology and the adult psychology where, in reality, identity reigns; viz.: in the region of the motives and conditions which make for mental power. The other is the assumption of likeness where marked difference is the feature most significant for educational purposes; I mean the specialization of aims and habits in the adult, compared with the absence of specialization in the child, and the connection of undifferentiated status with the full and free growth of the child.
>
> The adult is primarily a person with a certain calling and position in life. These devolve upon him certain specific responsibilities which he has to meet, and call into play certain formed habits. The child is primarily one whose calling is growth. He is concerned with arriving at specific ends and purposes instead of having a general framework already developed. He is engaged in forming habits rather than in definitely utilizing those already formed. Consequently he is absorbed in getting that all around contact with persons and things, that range of acquaintance with the physical and ideal factors of life, which shall afford the background and material for the specialized aims and pursuits of later life. He is, or should be, busy in the formation of a flexible variety of habits whose sole immediate criterion is their relation to full growth, rather than in acquiring certain skills whose value is measured by their reference to specialized technical accomplishments. This is the radical psychological and biological distinction, I take it, between the child and the adult. It is because of this distinction that children are neither physiologically nor mentally describable as "little men and women." (Pp. 66–67)

Today this view does not strike us as novel, let alone radical, but in 1899 Dewey's words could not have counted on a favorable reception, and few people would have grasped their significance for society's major institution, the school. But note that Dewey counterposes two sets of assumptions. Just as the assumptions he is challenging give one picture of what children are and should be, the assumptions Dewey prefers give a very different picture. The two sets of assumptions differ widely about what children are, but they are similar in that both say something about what children could or should be. Whatever the relationships between formal theory and practice, they reflect assumptions about what children should and can be. Such assumptions may turn out to be valid or invalid, harmful or enhancing, but they power theory and practice. What Dewey is saying is that in the real world in which we experience a problem—like the relationships between psychology and social practice in schools—the basis for theory and practice inevitably bears the imprint of shoulds and oughts and psychology cannot avoid dealing with the nature and consequences of that imprint. This is what Dewey means when he says, "The main point is whether the standpoint of psychological science, as a study of mechanism, is indifferent and opposed to the demands of education with its free interplay of personalities in their vital attitudes and aims".

Let us turn to Dewey's view of the relationship between theory and practice in schools as dictated by the contrasting assumptions:

> The narrow scope of the traditional elementary curriculum, the premature and excessive use of logical analytic methods, the assumption of ready-made faculties of observation, memory, attention, etc., which can be brought into play if only the child chooses to do so, the ideal of formal disciplines—all these find a large measure of their explanation in neglect of just this psychological distinction between the child and the adult. The hold of these affairs upon the school is so fixed that it is impossible to shake it in any fundamental way, excepting by a thorough appreciation of the actual psychology of the case. This appreciation cannot be confined to the educational leaders and theorists. No individual instructor can be sincere and whole hearted, to say nothing of intelligent, in carrying into effect the needed reforms, save as he genuinely understands the scientific basis and necessity of the change.
>
> But in another direction there is the assumption of fundamental difference: namely, as to the conditions which secure intellectual and moral progress and power. No one seriously questions that, with an adult, power and control are obtained through realization of personal ends and problems, through personal selection of means and materials which are relevant, and through personal adaptation and application of what is thus selected, together with whatever of experimentation and of testing is in-

volved in this effort. Practically every one of these three conditions of increase in power for the adult is denied for the child. For him problems and aims are determined by another mind. For him the material that is relevant and irrelevant is selected in advance by another mind. And, upon the whole, there is such an attempt to teach him a ready-made method for applying his material to the solution of his problems, or the reaching of his ends, that the factor of experimentation is reduced to the minimum. With the adult we unquestioningly assume that an attitude of personal inquiry, based upon the possession of a problem which interests and absorbs, is a necessary precondition of mental growth. With a child we assume that the precondition is rather the willing disposition which makes him ready to submit to any problem and material presented from without. Alertness is our ideal in one case; docility in the other. With one, we assume that power of attention develops in dealing with problems which make a personal appeal, and through personal responsibility for determining what is relevant. With the other we provide next to no opportunities for the evolution of problems out of immediate experience, and allow next to no free mental play for selecting, assorting and adapting the experiences and ideas that make for their solution. How profound a revolution in the position and service of text-book and teacher, and in methods of instruction depending therefrom, would be effected by a sincere recognition of the psychological identity of child and adult in these respects can with difficulty be realized.

Here again it is not enough that the educational commanders should be aware of the correct educational psychology. The rank and file, just because they are persons dealing with persons, must have a sufficient grounding in the psychology of the matter to realize the necessity and the significance of what they are doing. Any reform instituted without such conviction on the part of those who have to carry it into effect, would never be undertaken in good faith, nor in the spirit which its ideal inevitably demands; consequently it could lead only to disaster. (Pp. 67–68)

Dewey's description is, unfortunately, as appropriate today as it was in 1899.*

Having indicted prevailing theory and practice and offered a con-

---

*If things have not changed all that much in the intervening decades, during most of which Dewey was a dominant part of the educational scene, to what extent was Dewey's formulation of the issues at fault? In fact, Dewey failed to recognize that he had *created* his own educational setting and that he had not attempted to change an *existing* one. The setting he created lacked many of the features of the public schools he sought to influence. If he had attempted to introduce his ideas into other schools, he would have seen that his theory of education and his theory of institutional-social change were far from integrated (Sarason, 1971).

trasting view, Dewey anticipates the criticism that reconstructing educational theory and practice is the task not of the teacher but of the "general educational theorist," the middleman between the psychologist and the educational practitioner, who should formulate advice and rules for teacher action. To the extent, the criticism states, that the teacher acts on the basis of abstract psychological concepts of mechanism and personality, "he reduces persons to objects, and thereby distorts, or rather destroys, the ethical relationship which is the vital nerve of instruction." To these criticisms Dewey retorts:

> That there is some legitimate division of labor between the general educational theorist and the actual instructor, there is of course no doubt. As a rule, it will not be the one actively employed in instruction who will be most conscious of the psychological basis and equivalents of the educational work, nor most occupied in finding the pedagogical rendering of psychological facts and principles. Of necessity, the stress of interest will be elsewhere. But we have already found reason for questioning the possibility of making the somewhat different direction of interest into a rigid dualism of a legislative class on one side and an obedient subject class on the other. Can the teacher ever receive "obligatory prescriptions"? Can he receive from another a statement of the means by which he is to reach his ends, and not become hopelessly servile in his attitude? Would not such a result be even worse than the existing mixture of empiricism and inspiration?—just because it would forever fossilize the empirical element and dispel the inspiration which now quickens routine. Can a passive, receptive attitude on the part of the instructor (suggesting the soldier awaiting orders from a commanding general) be avoided, unless the teacher, as a student of psychology, himself sees the reasons and import of the suggestions and rules that are proferred him? (P. 69)

And then Dewey comes to the conceptual core of his address: the relationship among the psychological theorist, the educational scientist, and the practical worker? Between the theorist and the practical worker there is a "linking science." Between physics and the factory worker, Dewey says, is engineering; between natural science and the physician is scientific medicine. What lessons can be drawn from these examples that would guide us in thinking about the triad—psychological theorist, educational scientist, and teacher? Given the psychology of his time (and even ours), Dewey's answer is truly like a bolt out of the blue:

> The decisive matter is the extent to which the ideas of the theorist actually project themselves, through the kind offices of the middleman, into the

consciousness of the practitioner. It is the participation by the practical man in the theory, through the agency of linking science, that determines at once the effectiveness of the work done, and the moral freedom and personal development of the one engaged in it. It is because the physician no longer follows rules, which, however rational in themselves, are yet arbitrary to him (because grounded in principles that he does not understand), that his work is becoming liberal, attaining the dignity of a profession, instead of remaining mixture of empiricism and quackery. It is because, alas, engineering makes only a formal and not a real connection between physics and the practical workingmen in the mills that our industrial problem is an ethical problem of the most serious kind. The question of the amount of wages the laborer receives, of the purchasing value of this wage, of the hours and conditions of labor, are, after all, secondary. The problem primarily roots in the fact that the mediating science does not connect with his consciousness, but merely with his outward actions. He does not appreciate the significance and bearing of what he does; and he does not perform his work because of sharing in a larger scientific and social consciousness. If he did, he would be free. All other proper accompaniments of wage, and hours, healthful and inspiring conditions would be added unto him, because he would have entered into the ethical kingdom. Shall we seek an analogy with the teacher's calling in the workingmen in the mill, or in the scientific physician? (Pp. 67–70)

There are several remarkable features to Dewey's answer. The first is Dewey's obvious sensitivity to and knowledge of what was happening in his society. This was not the sensitivity of a bleeding heart but rather that of an astute observer of the social scene who understood that how a person regards himself and is regarded by others, his sense of competency, belonging, and relatedness, are not independent of where people are in the social order. No less important, Dewey never saw individuals out of a social context, be it a worker in a factory, a teacher or pupil in a classroom, or a child in a family; moreover, Dewey well understood that these "local," circumscribed contexts are themselves embedded in larger contexts (political, economic) that could be conceptualized in terms of structure, interrelatedness, ideology, and social history. In short, the social world possesses a structure no less complex than an individual's psychological structure.

The second remarkable feature of Dewey's remarks is the implication that psychological mechanisms and structure cannot be understood apart from the social context, especially when psychological theory about mechanism and structure purports to be relevant to real situations. The need for psychological theory arises because of questions and puzzles deriving from context (''out there'') and a theorist who forgets this simple fact is misleading himself: he leaves the questions unanswered and the puzzles unsolved. What Dewey implies here he subsequently makes crystal clear:

> The difficulties of psychological observation and interpretation are great enough in any case. We cannot afford to neglect any possible auxiliary. The great advantage of the Psycho-physical laboratory is paid for by certain obvious defects. The completer control of conditions, with resulting greater accuracy of determination, demands an isolation, a ruling out of the usual media of thought and action, which leads to a certain remoteness, and easily to a certain artificiality. When the results of laboratory experiment inform us, for example, that repetition is the chief factor influencing recall, we must bear in mind that the result is obtained with nonsense material—i.e., by excluding the conditions of ordinary memory. The result is pertinent if we state it thus: The more we exclude the usual environmental adaptations of memory the greater importance attaches to sheer repetition. It is dubious (and probably perverse) if we say: Repetition is the prime influence in memory.
>
> Now this illustrates a general principle. Unless our laboratory results are to give us artificialities, mere scientific curiosities, they must be subjected to interpretation by gradual reapproximation to conditions of life. The results may be very accurate, very definite in form; but the task of re-viewing them so as to see their actual import is clearly one of great delicacy and liability to error. The laboratory, in a word, affords no final refuge that enables us to avoid the ordinary scientific difficulties of forming hypotheses, interpreting results, etc. In some sense (from the very accuracy and limitations of its results) it adds to our responsibilities in this direction. (P. 75)

Dewey spoke thus in 1899. Almost three-quarters of a century later Cole, Hood, and McDermott (undated) at Rockefeller University circulated a monograph, *Ecological Niche Picking: Ecological Invalidity as an Axiom of Experimental Cognitive Psychology,* in which they incisively demonstrated the validity of Dewey's admonition.* Here is their abstract:

> The current state of theory in cognitive psychology is too weak a base to provide for principled means of making inferences from test and

---

*The three monographs (Cole, Hood, and McDermott, undated; Cole et al., undated) represent the joint labor of Cole and many of his colleagues at the Laboratory of Comparative Human Cognition and Institute for Comparative Human Development at the Rockefeller University.

laboratory-based observations to the wide variety of intellectual behavior observed in non-laboratory settings (everyday life). A review of cognitive research programs reveals several plausible speculations about thinking in everyday life based on laboratory research and theory. Descriptions of several everyday-life scenes drawn from our research with a group of children show these speculations to be plausible only if our descriptions and interpretations remain within the constraints of the model systems from which they were derived. But such models systematically suppress or exclude basic principles that our analysis suggests are fundamental to the organization of behavior, particularly the dynamically organized influence of individuals on their environment. We conclude that current method and theory of cognitive psychology are invalid for the non-laboratory settings to which many researchers wish to generalize. The need for developing alternative methods for describing scenes or task environments which people encounter in everyday life is emphasized. (P. 2)

I am not optimistic that this monograph and two others by Cole and his colleagues (undated) will have more impact than did Dewey's 1899 address.

Dewey would have been the last person to derogate the principle of experimentation, wherever it might be utilized. No psychologist had better knowledge (factual and conceptual) of the history and methods of science. And throughout his long life he never wavered in the belief that science (its spirit, morality, and traditions) represents the best means whereby human intelligence can pursue the formulation, analysis, and amelioration of the problems of social living. Science, for Dewey, was more than method or rigor. It was neither ritual nor game. Science aims to understand the nature of our world. It is that commitment that brings in its wake the "ordinary scientific difficulties of forming hypotheses, interpreting results, etc." What bothered Dewey about psychological theory and research was that in the mindless imitation of what was thought to be science psychology was unwittingly creating and elucidating an artificial world. It was a game and like all games it served to divert attention from the quotidian world.

In this respect (as in many others) Dewey and William James were of one mind. The reader will recall from the previous chapter James's reference to "those curious phenomena of dissociation of consciousness with which recent studies of hypnotic, hysteric and trance states have made us familiar, phenomena which surely threw more new light on human nature than the work of all psycho-physical laboratories put together.'' Neither James nor Dewey was advocating the philistine position that psychology has to have practical utility. What they were asserting was that if psychology is committed to understanding human behavior that exists only in the laboratory, it will mislead itself and society. Science, theory, and method are not at issue. The issue is whether psychology concerns itself with sense or nonsense, as Dewey so succinctly suggested in his comments about what is logically permissible to conclude about memory from studying nonsense syllables. In his three sentences about memory and nonsense syllables, Dewey, always the master logician, exposed the trap that psychology was setting for itself.

The third remarkable aspect of Dewey's thoughts on the relationship between theory and practice is the way he interrelates fact, assumption, and value. Psychological theory rests on conceptions about what man is and, therefore, about what man can be. The conceptions may be wrong, silly, vague, or circumscribed but they derive from a picture of what a person is, that is, how he or she or some part of the individual is put together, develops, and changes. In his address, as well as in all his other writings, Dewey spells out his conception of what man is and can be, and he explains why in testing these conceptions one has to look at the relationship between the structure of contexts and these conceptions. So, when Dewey looks at children in a classroom or laborers in a factory he sees social contexts that rest on assumptions that are in stark contrast to his assumptions about what man is or could be. Dewey looks at these contexts and can see why the people in them do what they do and appear to be capable of no more. But, Dewey argues, if you start with different assumptions about what man is and is capable of and change the context accordingly, people look and develop very differently. Dewey needed no instruction about the fact that theories and their implementation can be self-fulfilling, for good or for bad.

The assumption Dewey makes is that the fruitfulness and validity of a theory being tested in practice will, among other things, be a function of the degree to which there has been ''participation by the practical man in the theory.'' Today we hear a good deal about participation and about how important it is that all who will be affected by social action should have both knowledge about and a voice in the rationale for and implementation of the action. This may be a new idea to people today, but it was not new for Dewey. However, in his address he is emphasizing a somewhat different point: it is in the *self-interest* of the theorist whose ideas are being put into practice that the theory and the proposed implementation be understood and responded to by those who will be involved. Dewey took this seriously when he created the Laboratory School at the University of Chicago in 1896. Parents and teachers were collaborators and essential aids to Dewey both in the formulation of his ideas and in carrying them out. They were not "servile" recipients of an already completed formulation and plan of action. Far from being a token gesture, his relationship to these collaborators bespoke a genuine respect for and need of them. At one point Dewey says about the relation between psychology and education: "While the psychological theory would guide and illuminate the practice, acting upon the theory would immediately test it, and thus criticize it, bringing about its revision and growth. In the large and open sense of the words psychology becomes a working hypothesis; the result is both greater practical control and continued growth in theory." Dewey's contribution inheres in the insight that concepts like theory and practice imply a dichotomy that impoverishes both theory and practice, a point that years later an eminent theorist and experimental psychologist stated and illustrated clearly and persuasively (Garner, 1972). Whereas Dewey was presenting a point of view he thought psychology should adopt, Garner convincingly demonstrated that the necessity to solve problems of practice has great impact on psychological theory in the "hard" parts of psychology. I cannot refrain from quoting Garner's Dewey-like words:

> There is a fable, carefully nurtured over the centuries by the basic scientists, particularly those who see basic as pure, about the relation between the scientist who acquires information and the problem solver who applies that information. The fable is that scientists acquire the knowledge, that this knowledge goes into the public domain, and that when a problem solver needs some knowledge to solve his problem, he extracts it from the public domain, uttering words of gratitude as he does so, and solves his problem. The actuality that the scientist has provided knowledge needed by the problem solver occurs in some mysterious fashion. Mysterious though the process is, it is so effective that no tampering must be allowed, and in fact, the less contact the scientist has with the problems of the problem solver, the more apt he will be to fill the public domain with knowledge of ultimately greatest import to the problem solver. This

is the fable, but like all fables, it is a myth. It does not work that way at
all. (P. 942)

It does not work that way at all for psychologists like Garner, who
manage to transcend the world view their socialization and education
has inculcated in them.*

The fourth remarkable feature of Dewey's address is similar to the
third but emphasis shifts from the self-interest of the theorist in
developing and appropriately testing theory to the ethical aspects of
the theory-practice process. Dewey has a clear picture not only of what
man is and can be but also of what he should be; the latter is implicit
in the former. It is evident to Dewey that any view of what man is and
can be necessarily dictates what man should be.

The theorist may be unaware of this point, may disclaim any interest in these ethical implications, and may even resent the ethical in-
ferences others draw from his psychological theory, but these attitudes
deal with the issue by avoiding it. And the issue can be put this way:
has there ever been a theory that purported to explain human behavior
that was independent of the theorist's implicit, unchallenged world
view of what man is, can be, and should be? My reading of these explanations, from the Greeks to the present day, gives a negative
answer. Over the milliennia each theorist has justified his explanations
in part as a reaction to the errors and inadequacies of other theorists'
pictures of what man is, can be, and should be. Each theorist responds
not only to the explicit substance of past (or competing) theories but
also to unrecognized, time and place determined assumptions of what
man is, can be, and should be. In short, psychological theories do not
have virgin births, i.e., unsullied by the social genetics of the time. So,
when Dewey introduces ethics into the theory-practice process, he is
confronting, not avoiding, the issue. He is telling us the ethical implications he draws for the process. Whether he is right or wrong in the
specific implications is not the point. The point is that when Dewey

* It might seem that the arguments I am presenting in this book are appropriate, or
most applicable, to the "softer" parts of psychology. This is not my position at all.
Phenomenologically speaking, every psychologist has a picture of what man is and
should be, of what society is or should be, and this picture infiltrates (indeed, is in part
the basis of) his or her theories, along with the psychologist's way of thinking about
theory and practice. How one thinks about theory and practice reflects how one sees
one's self in the social order, i.e., how the social order *should* be organized and the different worths that different people *should have* in such an order.

says there is an ethical problem of the worst kind when the engineer "makes only a formal and not a real connection between physics and the practical workingmen in the mills" he is contrasting two very different conceptions of what man is, can be, and should be. And he is cautioning the psychological theorist to recognize, not to skirt, the ethical question.

Dewey could not conceive of a psychology apart from the society in which it is embedded, an embeddedness that has to be viewed historically. At the end of his address, when Dewey returns to the ethical issue, he,makes the point that when morality and laws derive from custom, the means for their realization also are given by custom: "So long as social values are determined by instinct and habit, there is no conscious question as to the method of their achievement, *and hence no need of psychology*" (italics added). It is when moral ideals and laws

> are in any way divorced from habit and tradition, when they are consciously proclaimed, there must be some substitute for custom as an organ of execution. We must know the method of their operation and know it in detail. . . . the fact that conscious, as distinct from customary, morality and psychology have had a historic parallel march, is just the concrete recognition of the necessary equivalence between ends consciously conceived, and interest in the means upon which the ends depend. We have the same reality stated twice over: once as value to be realized, and once as mechanism of realization. . . . when once the values come to consciousness, when once a Socrates insists upon the organic relation of a reflective life and morality, then the means, the machinery by which ethical ideals are projected and manifested, comes to consciousness also. Psychology must needs be born as soon as morality becomes reflective. (P. 77)

Born to serve what purpose? To account for the "mechanisms or workings of personality"? Dewey's answer returns him to the unanswered question with which he began his address: what is the relation of psychology to the social sciences?

To repeat, Dewey was not against the laboratory or any research focus or method that promised to contribute to knowledge. No one more than he defended the scientist's right to go where his ideas and interests take him. His warning to psychology was threefold. First, if you purport that your theories and findings have significance for social practice, it is incumbent upon you to demonstrate that the conditions of research from which your findings derive approximate the conditions of actual social living. Second, the self-interest of the theorist should lead him to recast the role of all who are involved in the theory-practice process. Third, the ethical aspects of the theory-practice process stem not from ex cathedra considerations but inhere in the psychological theory that explicitly departs from a view of man that derives from custom, habit, and tradition. Departure from the unreflective, "customary" psychology (from Plato and Aristotle to Freud and Skinner) inevitably raises both new conceptions about man and social living and new ethical considerations. *"Psychology must needs be born as soon as morality becomes reflective."* (italics added).

"I make no apology for presenting this discussion to an Association of Psychologists rather than to a gathering of educators." We do not know the response of his audience in 1899 but we do know that Dewey figures not at all in the subsequent history of psychology. Psychology pigeonholed him as educator and philosopher and therefore felt no need to deal with the substance of his thinking. For an explanation one can turn to Dewey's Gifford lectures at the University of Edinburgh in 1929. The lectures were later published as *The Quest for Certainty* (1960), as tightly reasoned, historically based, probing, and challenging a book as I have ever read, dealing with changes in modes of consecutive investigation in science and philosophy from the prescientific analysis of the classic period and Middle Ages to the ways of thought characteristic of modern science and philosophy. Of particular interest here is the first chapter in which Dewey asks: "What is the cause and the import of the sharp division between theory and practice. Why should the latter be disesteemed along with matter and the body?" (p. 5). The gist of Dewey's answer follows:

> There is no need to expatiate upon the risk which attends overt action. The burden of proverbs and wise saws is that the best laid plans of men as of mice gang agley. Fortune rather than our own intent and act determines eventual success and failure. The pathos of unfulfilled expectation, the tragedy of defeated purpose and ideals, the catastrophes of accident, are the commonplaces of all comment on the human scene. We survey conditions, make the wisest choice we can; we act, and we must trust the rest to fate, fortune or providence. Moralists tell us to look to the end when we act and then inform us that the end is always uncertain. Judging, planning, choice, no matter how prudently executed, never are the sole determinants of any outcome. Alien and indifferent natural forces, unforeseeable conditions enter in and have a decisive voice. The more important the issue, the greater is their say as to the ulterior event.

Hence men have longed to find a realm in which there is an activity which is not overt and which has no external consequences. "Safety first" has played a large role in effecting a preference for knowing over doing and making. With those to whom the process of pure thinking is congenial and who have the leisure and the aptitude to pursue their preference, the happiness attending knowing is unalloyed; it is not entangled in the risks which overt action cannot escape. Thought has been alleged to be a purely inner activity, intrinsic to mind alone; and according to traditional classic doctrine, "mind" is complete and self-sufficient in itself. Overt action may follow upon its operations but in an external way, a way not intrinsic to its completion. Since rational activity is complete within itself it needs no external manifestation. Failure and frustration are attributed to the accidents of an alien, intractable and inferior realm of existence. The outer lot of thought is cast in a world external to it, but one which in no way injures the supremacy and completeness of thought and knowledge in their intrinsic natures. (Pp. 7–8)

Action in the world "out there" is messy, far from controllable, an obstacle course that will not go away and will not bend to one's perfected theories. As in so many other areas, the Greeks first identified this problem:

The realms of knowledge and action were each divided into two regions. It is not to be inferred that Greek philosophy separated activity from knowing. It connected them. But it distinguished activity from action—that is, from making and doing. Rational and necessary knowledge was treated, as in the celebrations of it by Aristotle, as an ultimate, self-sufficient and self-enclosed form of self-originated and self-conducted activity. It was ideal and eternal, independent of change and hence of the world in which men act and live, the world we experience perceptibly and practically. "Pure activity" was sharply marked off from practical action. The latter, whether in the industrial or the fine arts, in morals or in politics, was concerned with an inferior region of Being in which change rules, and which accordingly has Being only by courtesy, for it manifests deficiency of sure footing in Being by the fact of change. It is infected with non-being. (P. 17–18)

What Dewey goes on to do is to expose the axioms and pictures of this world view, which has been held from the Greeks down to the present day. And that includes the psychologists of his time. The world view of these psychologists was, of course, not identical to that of the Greeks but in one respect there is similarity: the belief that practice and action are not of equal importance with theory. The latter is basic, the former is applied; the latter is pure and ideal, uncluttered by the vicissitudes and vagaries of ordinary living, the former contains error, noise, and capriciousness; the latter is a product of the rational mind, the former is God knows what. Those actions are justifiable that derive from perfected theory; otherwise action should be postponed. In short, you act only after the problems have been "solved" in theory. And, as Dewey cautions in his address, do not confuse theory's simulated, experimental activity in the laboratory with action or practice in the social world. For Dewey, the theory-practice dichotomy is false and misleading.

It is no wonder that psychologists dealt with Dewey by ignoring him: he was challenging part of the core of their world view. But there was another, related part of that core that Dewey was challenging: the relation between psychological theory and political ideologies. A theory about human behavior, Dewey asserted, could not be independent of the ideological foundations of a society and the psychologist's place in that social order. It is noteworthy that Dewey's point was cited by another president of the American Psychological Association in 1939 (Allport, 1978), a year in which the specter of the triumph of Nazism came into the consciousness of the Western world. American psychologists, like their predecessors in World War I, whom Yerkes (1978) discussed, were forced to recognize that *their* psychology stood in a particular relation to *their* society. Their society was in them and their theories and research. So, it was not fortuitous that Gordon Allport in his APA presidential address in 1939 reminded his audience of John Dewey:

> Speaking on this very campus forty years ago, John Dewey, later to become the eighth president of our Association, made what for that time was a striking observation. Psychology, he held, cannot help but be politically conditioned. He had in mind, for example, the fact that doctrines of the fixedness of human nature flourish in an aristocracy and perish in a democracy. The privileges of the elite in ancient Greece, and for psychological theories of their day. Under modern conditions theories of statehood play a major role. (P. 393)

Allport goes on to illustrate the wisdom of Dewey's early observation:

> The president of the Deutsche Gesellschaft, addressing that organization last year, praised typological studies that enabled psychology, in matters

of heredity, race, and education, to pick out the national Gegentypus whose unwelcome qualities are individualism and intellectualism. In passing, he warned against using the mental tests that one of the great figures in psychology, William Stern, a Jew, had introduced, and said that he wondered not at all that some of his colleagues had been censured for pursuing a prerevolutionary course of thought. At the same time he added:

"Antagonistic foreign countries speak of coordination (Gleichschaltung) whenever conformity of science and politics is perceived. No, this conformity is certainly not based on coordination, but upon the fact that politics and science, now for the first time, strive after truth even in the basic questions of existence, over which heretofore darkness and error reigned."

And what is the situation with us? Do we American psychologists lack politically determined attitudes? At first thought it would seem so, for are we not entirely free in our individual researches, and may we not hold any fantastic view that we choose? We may, and that proves the point for the political determinist, for only in a democracy can anything like a "socially detached intelligentsia" be realized. On the theory that democracy will ultimately gain by giving each thinker all the space he wants, we American Psychologists are subsidized, encouraged, and defended. Each worker may elect, as he pleases, any section or subsection of psychology that he finds suited to his taste and abilities. (P. 393)

In one respect Allport confirms the wisdom of Dewey's observation that psychology is politically conditioned. In another respect, Allport unwittingly confirms Dewey's views about the potency of the implicit basis for the honoring of theory over practice. Why does Allport put quotation marks around the words "socially detached intelligentsia" if not to convey the primary importance one should attach to detached thought and theory? Dewey would agree with Allport that "each worker may elect, as he pleases, any section or subsection of psychology that he finds suited to his taste and abilities," but he would not agree with Allport that to be socially detached, to be free from dealing with the social contexts for which one's theory and research are supposed to be appropriate, is necessarily conducive to the growth of theory. To want to be free in this way is at the same time to be imprisoned in a world view that honors theory and disesteems practice, a view that Dewey showed leads down the road to failure.

Allport was well acquainted with Dewey's writings and it is not surprising that he thought of him as World War II approached. Ironically, the war years dramatically confirmed Dewey's position on the theory-practice dichotomy because a generation of psychologists eagerly plunged into war related action that changed them and their theories. They were no longer "detached" and they were inevitably confronted with the adequacy of their theories for problems in naturally occurring contexts. Garner (1972) has given examples of psychologists whose theories changed dramatically in the course of their war related actions. It is unfortunate but not surprising (given psychology's ahistorical stance) that the story of how World War II transformed psychologists and their theories has not been written because that story would flesh out Garner and Dewey's point that the basic-applied and theory-practice dichotomies are false in conception and mischievous in their consequences. But that conclusion was not clearly drawn by most psychologists, and following the war, as I indicated in an earlier chapter, psychology again set theory above practice. It is true that as never before psychologists became interested in social problems and public policies but that interest took two major forms: convincing policymakers that the support of basic research is the best investment a society can make if it "really" wants sound "solutions" to social problems; and serving as consultants to agencies and policymakers in order to bring current theory and research findings to bear on specific problems. Interested but detached consultants. On the other hand, there were psychologists in increasing numbers who sought and gained employment in the public and private sectors and in whom the seeds of disillusionment with psychological theory (and their education in psychology) were taking root. This did not necessarily mean they were ineffective in their work but rather that they could not easily avoid the thought that what they had been taught was either wrong or a gross oversimplification. As one such very effective person once said to me when I asked him about the relationship between what he thought and did, on the one hand, and the psychological theories and research findings that were presumably appropriate to his responsibilities, on the other hand, he replied: "Fortunately, and for reasons I do not understand, early on I realized that I had to unlearn what I had been taught."

In an earlier chapter I discussed the current malaise in the social sciences generally and in psychology particularly, relating this sense to puzzlement and disillusionment about the discrepancy between the hopes and promises of the sixties and the accomplishments. Wherein were we wrong? What were we ignorant of? How did we mislead ourselves? Why did what seemed to be a golden opportunity end up a tarnished, bitter memory? These are the questions psychologists and others ask themselves. There are, of course, no simple answers but any serious answer would have to center around the issues posed by Dewey in his 1899 address and pursued by him in almost all of his subsequent writings. It is deserving of special emphasis that Dewey's discussion of psychology and social practice is rooted in a perception of the ways in which our society is organized and works, the conflicting value systems it contains, and the social-historical matrix from which it developed and whose influence continues in the present. Psychology is social psychology but the adjective ''social'' refers to more than what we ordinarily mean by situations, environment, interpersonal reactions, or group processes and interactions. When we travel to a foreign land and someone asks us where we come from, we say America or the United States; we do not say we are from Utah or Connecticut or Arizona. And in the answer we give we intuitively know that we are conveying distinctive features of our psychological makeup, features that singly may not be distinctive but in their combination are. We rarely pursue how these features become part of us (we possess them as much as they possess us), or why people differ in how these features are organized in them, or why those who came before us differed from us. We know that we were made, so to speak, in this society but what do we mean by "this society"? As Dewey stressed, as long as our thinking and actions are determined by and congruent with custom and tradition, there is no spur to self-reflection and therefore to understanding how the society is in us. But once incongruence is experienced (as it was in the sixties, in the Great Depression, in the Civil War, and in the years preceding the American Revolution) "morality becomes reflective" and "psychology must needs be born." It is in such times of incongruence that we realize that the abstraction "society," about which we did not have to think because we assumed we understood it, has structural and ideological characteristics to which we literally "paid no mind." When psychology is born or reborn it comes from the womb of society. If we recognize this point but shrink from pursuing its significance, that says as much about the hold of tradition on thought as it does about the difficulty of the task.

For all practical purposes, Dewey had no influence on the development of psychology. Yet his 1899 address is more relevant to the malaise that so many psychologists feel today than any other paper I have read. Bear in mind that the malaise is a direct consequence of psychologists' efforts in social practice. No one coerced psychologists to engage in these efforts; they sought this arena as much as they were made welcome in it. They did not regard themselves as do-gooders, a derisive epithet they applied to those who, Don Quixote style, seek to remedy the world's ills with no conception of the difficulty of the task and armed only with the best of intentions. Today, however, more than a few psychologists look back and see themselves as having kinship with the do-gooders—more sophisticated perhaps, but equally ineffectual. Why ineffectual? That is the question that plagues them and it is the question they do not know how to approach, let alone answer.

Dewey, in his 1899 address, suggests some of the aspects that an answer would have to encompass. One aspect involves a radical recasting of the theory-practice dichotomy, a recasting that has had, and will continue to have, enormous obstacles to overcome because it challenges age-old distinctions between theory and practice. Another aspect (muted in the 1899 address but center stage in Dewey's other writings) is the organic relation between the substance of psychology and the social history from which that psychology has emerged. Not the history of the field or of a particular issue in it, but a history that tries to see the substance of the field in terms of the ideology and structure of an interrelationship among the society's major institutions—political, economic, scientific, religious, educational. To put it briefly, to see social history as a series of transformations in world views each of which has defined man, society, and the world. The third aspect derives from the second and requires on the part of the psychologist a heightened realization that, like everyone else, he or she is a product of time and place and that everyone else should be accorded the respect that the psychologist wants accorded to himself or herself. If any one word epitomizes Dewey's view of people it is *respect*—respect not only for what they do but also for what they can learn to do; respect not only for what they are but also for what they can be. Respect is not a common word in psychology's literature and yet this word became a rallying point in recent decades for important segments of our society who resented and fought against what they saw as disrespectful conceptions of themselves. Psychologists (among many others, of course) were attitudinally and conceptually unprepared to understand, let alone deal with, such militancy. They thought they understood their society but they were wrong. They thought their psychology was appropriate to social realities, that it not only mirrored those realities but also contained the basis for altering them in desirable ways. But, as Dewey said about permissible generalizations from laboratory studies that fail to approximate naturally occurring situations, psychology had mired itself in a tradition on the basis of which it had created an artificial world within which it was comfortable and productive, *until it ventured forth into the world of daily living.*

These aspects, particularly the first two, will be the most difficult for psychology to accept. To recast the theory-practice dichotomy requires changing one's values about theory and practice and giving up mindless devotion to familiar methodologies and modes of analysis, as well as changing the sites and conditions of one's work. What is involved is no less than ceasing to ape the so-called hard sciences. The issue is not where and how one conducts research (as if in the abstract one can prescribe a methodology) but whether the conditions approximate the naturally occurring context from which the problem arose and to which an answer is sought. When Dewey talks about "gradual approximations" to the naturally occurring context he is not asking for immediate relevance and he is not in principle criticizing studies that are in some important respects dissimilar to the naturally occurring context, as long as the limits this sets on permissible generalizations are recognized.

It is understandable that psychologists will resist the obligations of the social historical stance. As one of my students said: "You are asking for too much. You want us to be psychologists *and* social historians, and we're having trouble finding the time to learn what we are supposed to learn just to be psychologists. You are also implying that we have to learn something about the political and economic basis and structure of society. You want us to be renaissance people." In later pages I shall deal at some length with this argument, but the gist of it can be presented here: to be a psychologist, to be a student of human mind and behavior, is to indulge both courage and arrogance, courage because it requires a degree of self-searching and understanding that we ask of no one in any other field, and arrogance because it suggests that one can transcend in one's self all of the consequences of those factors and dynamics that we know spur, shape, and distort how other people think, talk, and act. We know that such transcendence is partial at best and so we rely on methodologies to control for our imperfections. We remove as much of ourselves as possible in order not unwittingly to distort the data we obtain and analyze. Such efforts are necessary and commendable as long as it is kept clearly in mind that the methods psychologists invent, no less than any other invention like TV, space shuttles, or transistors, are cultural products. They are responses to a problem that the inventor *and* others in the society deem worthy of solution. The invention has a history that antedates the inventor. And like any other invention, a psychological method is viewed as appropriate to what people are, or to what they can learn to do, or to what they will find interesting, or to what they want, or to what they can reveal.

Psychological methods, in short, derive from a time and place based conception of what people are or can be. They are socially sanctioned, a fact that becomes evident only when the society bans a particular method or severely restricts its use. At these times we recognize in the methods we invent and employ an ethical-moral component. It is illusory, therefore, for the psychologist to think that his methods are controls against personal and cultural bias. Be it an intelligence test or an automatic ice cube maker, it is a cultural artifact that says something important both about how people in the society see themselves and each other and about what is desirable. When a method is seen as but a technical means to achieve certain ends, the very problem that stimulated the invention of the method reappears in the latter. Needless to say, I am not arguing against method or control but against the wholesale failure of psychology to see that method and technique inevitably contain the very problem they are intended to circumvent. As I replied to my student:

> You really do not have a choice about trying to understand your culture, how it shaped you and the social historical context that is background to your here and now, much of which is, in fact, still in your here and now. You will not comprehend what is involved by studying an ahistorical, acultural psychology. But as soon as you begin to sense that something is wrong and horribly incomplete in your education and training, then, in Dewey's terms, a new psychology needs to be born. If that should hap-

pen, it will not be because of you, me, and others, although we will be part of the story, but because the relationship between society and psychology as an institution will have been recognized as problematic by both sides. That relationship is now problematic. From within and without psychology there is a sense that something is wrong. But that is true for all the social sciences. What would really be surprising would be if it were true only for psychology. Now, what would you predict would be the most prepotent response of establishment psychology? Would you not predict that it would conclude that it had not been true to its basic traditions, that it had faddishly been diverted from mining the ores of basic theory and research, that it had willingly been seduced into doing more than it was capable of, that we should postpone any further involvement in the "practical problems" of social living, that we should give up trying to change a world that needs fundamental knowledge and not half-assed advice, that we should leave practical problems to practical people? But why would you make such a prediction? After all, these people are not faddists. They are, in fact, extraordinarily capable and creative people. Can you explain the difference in outlook between you and them in terms of an individual psychology, e.g., Skinner, Freud, Maslow, etc.?"

There is another but related part of the answer to my student and it has to do with a problem Dewey raised at the beginning of his 1899 address but felt unprepared to deal with: the relation of psychology to the other social sciences. But from his discussion of a special instance of that problem, the relation of psychology to education (which Dewey regarded as a social science), we can infer the outlines of what he might have said. Dewey was always suspicious of dichotomies, e.g., theory-practice, individual-society, psychology-education, the laboratory–the real world, so-called. He would not look at each of the social sciences as separate areas of knowledge having distinct relationships with or implications for practice. Each of the social sciences depends upon and requires the others. Each of them is not an element in a whole called social science, because if that were the case the whole would be less than the sum of its parts. We would like to believe that the whole would be (should be) greater than the sum of its parts but that can come about not by addition but only by integration. That integration will not be achieved by happenstance.

Just as the enlargement of theory comes about through its integrated relationship to, and testing by, practice, and practice is challenged and altered by the stimulus of theory, so the desirable inter-relationship between psychology and the social sciences will come about only through a process in which they are used together. But how can that happen when each social science treasures its distinctiveness if not superiority (as does theorist over practitioner)? How can it happen when in the university each of the social sciences is administratively autonomous and fights tooth and nail for its separateness? Since World War II we have heard much about the need for interdisciplinary education and research, and many efforts have been made to achieve that end. They have not added up to much, partly because such efforts have been based on addition and not on integration. More important has been the failure of each of the social sciences to start from the one problem they have in common: *each is as much a creation of the society as it is a shaper of that society; each in relation to society is as much effect as cause.* Seen in this way, every social science must deal not only with the nature of the society but also with the development of means for diluting the consequences of its conceptual imprisonment in the nature of that society. When this communality is perceived by the social sciences, the possibility for integration will exist. It will be less a matter of shared values than of shared problems. It will be less a matter of shared successes than of the perception of shared failures.

CHAPTER VII

NICHE AND BIAS IN THE SOCIAL ORDER

THEORY AND PRACTICE, the individual and society: psychology, I have been suggesting, has been oriented to these dichotomies in self-defeating ways. This is not to say that these dichotomies are unnecessary or unproductive and that we had best be rid of them. That would be to throw the baby out with the bathwater. The problem has been that in uncritically accepting and sustaining these dichotomies psychology did throw the baby out with the bathwater. By separating theory from practice, by valuing theory over practice, psychology did not have to confront the possibility that its substance and findings had little or no validity for the social world, a criterion by which psychology explicitly wanted to be judged. Psychology justified itself by what it could contribute to society, but psychology steered a course that long delayed recognizing that it was seriously off course. And by concentrating almost exclusively on the contents, processes, and dynamics of the individual mind, psychology never had to deal seriously with how the structure and traditions of society shape the individual mind, *including that of the psychologist.*

Of course, psychology recognized that the human organism is inevitably social, that it operates in a social medium, but social referred to very circumscribed contexts (interpersonally and physically) whose relationships to the larger society concerned psychology very little. Psychological theory was about individuals, not about individuals and

146

society. There was, consequently, no need for the psychologist to be self-conscious about the degree to which his or her behavior derived from his or her development and place in the larger and structured society. Psychology, of course, was very sensitive to how the psychologist's passions and mind set can unwittingly, selectively, and insidiously influence observations and analysis of data. In shaping itself to the scientific tradition and mold, psychology was quite aware of the importance of controlling for the imperfections of the psychologist. Psychology became agonizingly self-conscious about the problem of control and this led to an emphasis on controlled experimentation, i.e., on methodology that would protect data from the influences of the psychologist's human frailties. The problem was, of course, not peculiar to experimentation. Freud's descriptions and conceptualizations about transference and countertransference in the clinical situation underlined both the generality and the complexity of controlling for personal bias.

The merits of this self-consciousness about the problem of control require no elaboration here. What does require elaboration is that this self-consciousness is rooted in and derives from an individual psychology. That is to say, bias is ubiquitous, a characteristic or potentiality of every individual. The nature and strength of the bias may differ from individual to individual, if only because each individual is unique. From the standpoint of science one cannot deal with these individual differences except by devising methodologies that make it impossible for these differences to become operative in data collection and analysis.

But what about the substance of the ideas, concepts, or theories that antedate the research? Clearly, they are not ubiquitous. And, equally clearly, we do not regard them as ahistorical, random products of individual minds. We make the assumption that the shape and thrust of the substantive formulations have diverse sources not all of which, by any means, are known to the formulator. I am not here referring to unconscious sources, i.e., to forgotten or repressed ideas or events that are idiosyncratically related to the conscious formulation.* What I am referring to is that the formulators occupy a certain place and role in a structured society, by virtue of which role and place their

*If I were referring to unconscious sources that would be another example of pursuing understanding through a quintessentially individual psychology, and each individual formulation would require a separate case study.

outlook and behavior have been shaped. As a group, they have under-
gone a socialization process. We may call the process education or
training: a long series of rites of passage that make them eligible for
certain roles in certain places. It is a process in which self, others, and
the nature of the society get defined. It is, of course, a continuation of
a process that begins at birth. They do not come to their "higher"
education without their society already being in them. The more pro-
longed, systematic, and effective the socialization, the less self-
conscious people are about the different factors and forces that shaped
them. To be socialized means that one has absorbed and accom-
modated to predetermined conceptions of the way things are and
ought to be. One may resist and resent the process but if one wants to
occupy a certain place and role in the society (e.g., lawyer, physician,
psychologist) one has to traverse successfully the rites of passage. The
socialization may be partial but its effects are never absent. For most
people the process is far more than partial; it is so successful that for all
practical purposes there is no questioning, no self-consciousness, about
the forces that shaped them and their conception of their society. The
lack of this type of self-consciousness is no less a source of bias in the
psychologist than the distortion-producing motivations that he
possesses like everyone else. This is especially the case when the aim of
the psychologist is to understand and/or change some aspect of
people's lives. In earlier chapters I illustrated this point in connection
with the use and applications of psychological tests; the theoreticians
seemed to be not at all self-conscious that they were a special group in
this society: "native" Americans, White, Protestant, highly educated
and trained in elite universities, and economically privileged. They did
not see any of these characteristics as sources of bias in their theorizing
and research. Nor did they see that where they worked, in universities
(by no means random in selection), as possibly influencing the substance of their thinking. None of these factors had to be confronted and
efforts to transcend them made. How can you confront and transcend
that which you do not consider in any way problematic?

That it was not problematic testifies to the effectiveness of
psychologists' socialization, during which process they assimilated
(among other things) conceptions about what this society was, is, and
should be, how it is structured, the aims of education, the determinants of people's social-economic-cultural status and accomplishments, and the relationships between science and society, between the

university and society. That these conceptions may not have been wholly "objective"; that their factual basis may not have been all that factual; that their picture of society and its myriad groups and institutions derived from limited direct experience; that it was easier to state and test their conceptions than to excavate and control for omnipresent preconceptions; that their recommendations for practice and action would have unintended as well as intended consequences; and that they were far more knowledgeable about how theory should relate to and influence practice than about how theory did relate to and influence practice—there was precious little self-consciousness among psychologists about these sources of bias, error, and distortion. Psychologists saw themselves as representatives of science, not as representatives of a special social-economic-ethnic group that did not develop randomly or occupy a random niche in society. They were, of course, representatives of both but they could not see that by virtue of the stated aim of psychology to understand man in society they faced a special, unavoidable problem: what might be the relationship between the substance of psychologists' theories, on the one hand, and their outlook and perspective derived from their social development, on the other? How can one assume—what evidence is there in the history of man—that a person's conceptions of man and society are independent of his or her development and place in society? But that question is precisely the one that psychologists managed to avoid asking, largely because of their exclusive concern with being paragons of the scientific community. But the sciences that psychology wanted to emulate did not have man and society as their central subject matter. Nevertheless, these sciences revealed a good deal about how one could not trust scientists (and everyone else) to keep passions and practices separate. At the core of science is the commandment "Thou shalt not allow passion, prejudice, and preconception to alter or distort what you do, explain, and report." It might be better put thus: "Thou shalt not forget that thou shalt not indulge known human imperfections." But a correlated commandment has to be formulated: "Thou shalt not forget that one always starts with a picture of man in society that inevitably reflects where one has been and is in that society, a picture containing valid and invalid, perspective constraining, perspective distorting, prophecy fulfilling characteristics."

In our everyday lives we understand aspects of this commandment very well. If you are a factory worker, not only do you know that management and the owners see the world differently from you, but you also assume that these differences are not independent of where you and they come from and are in the society. That is to say, you know that the differences are not merely a matter of individual variation. And, of course, if you are the owners and management, you make similar assumptions. These pictures, these informal theories, govern action, i.e., theory and practice are not dichotomized in daily living. And it is almost always the case that these theories essentially never change, although they may get more rigid and complicated. There is no need to multiply examples. But how should we think about psychologists in these respects? On the surface it would appear that psychologists are so diverse in what they do and where they work that it makes no sense to talk about them as a group having certain outlooks that govern their perceptions of other groups, which in turn perceive psychologists in special ways. As I already indicated, earlier in this century psychologists were far more homogeneous than today in terms of socioeconomic background, religion, ethnicity, gender, color, education, and site of work (the university). Unlike factory workers, they did not see themselves in an adversarial relationship to other groups in society. They saw themselves as part of the scientific community, as contributors to the society's welfare, and as educators of the society's youth. What was good for psychology was good for society. When several decades later the head of General Motors said that what was good for his company was good for the country, I assume that most psychologists, like a lot of other people, snorted at this artless denial of any self-serving interest. Like the chairman of General Motors, psychology had no conceptual way of entertaining the possibility that its view of itself and society was politically and socially conditioned. It all seemed obvious even though there was much in psychology that demonstrated that what people see as obvious is frequently wrong or even dangerously misleading.

In 1936 a book was published that is very relevant to the present discussion. It is J. F. Brown's *Psychology and the Social Order*. The book is unusual, if not unique, in several respects. Its author was extraordinarily knowledgeable about Gestalt, psychoanalytic, and Marxist theories; the book is no less than a systematic effort to integrate the writings of Lewin, Freud, and Karl Marx, none of whom at the time was anywhere near the mainstream of American psychology. The book was written as a text in social psychology. It is fascinating but not easy reading; it is quite the opposite of any attempt to popularize the contributions of Lewin, Freud, and Marx. The author, on the faculty of the University of Kansas, regarded American psychology, especially social psychology, as having little or nothing to say about man in society. The book was stimulated by the conclusion that a psychology that did not come to grips with what the Great Depression and European fascism signified for man in society (past, present, and future) was at best a charade and at worst a disgraceful example of irresponsibility. Brown does not offer the reader a program for action but rather a way of conceptualizing social behavior and societal change. He was no slavish partisan of Lewin, Freud, or Marx, just as he was no thoughtless critic of American psychology. I venture to say that more than any other psychology book of its time or before Brown's text touched on problems that forced their way into the world agenda only in the post–World War II era.

For my present purposes the following statement by Brown is quite relevant:

> In a great deal that is written on social classes it is quite obvious that very definite and precise wishes are often the fathers of very indefinite and hazy thoughts. This is certainly true of most of the bourgeois apologists for capitalism and preachers of cooperation; it is decidedly true of great sections of Pareto's *The Mind and Society,* the one bourgeois attempt at a truly scientific sociology, and it is true of many single Marxist analyses. With few exceptions those who deny or gloss over the problems of classes and the class struggle, dynamically have membership-character in groups which would ultimately stand to lose a great deal by the class struggle, did it exist. And in these groups must be reckoned certain individuals who pay lip service to the cause of the workers but whose actual bread is very thickly buttered by the capitalist system and whose fare would be crusts alone under any other. . . . On the other hand, those (there are individual exceptions here, of course, too) who most vehemently insist that the class struggle is basic to all contemporary politics, social philosophy, and economic theory would have the most to gain from a successfully conceived and executed proletarian uprising. This fact alone, looked on from the standpoint of a "disinterested" scientist, gives considerable support to the Marxist position. One of our chief conclusions in this work will be that membership-character in a social field is the chief single determiner of the individual's aims and ambitions, his fears and hopes. It has also been shown that threatened destruction of an organized social group increases the degree of organization for group self-protection.

Since it is the avowed aim of the Marxist practical program to destroy the capitalists as a class and to further the class struggle, it is scarcely surprising that apologists for the existing order begin by denying antipathies to it, sometimes even denying the existence of classes themselves. Unpleasant thoughts about ourselves, as the Freudians have shown, tend to be pushed into the background. Naturally the comfortable bourgeois denies the "class struggle." Even the Marxists do not expect him to affirm it. . . .

> In this vast confusion of rival opinions the "academic" social scientist is inclined to hold his tongue, because he pretends a neutral disinterested attitude and protests that social science is not yet in a position to solve such problems. I cannot refrain from pointing out that such a glossing over of this highly important problem is quite indicative of academic "social science." The position of the scientist in both endowed and state tax-supported institutions depends not only in the long but also in the short run on the existing social order. His membership-character is in the bourgeois region and consequently he usually does not even so much as mention the class struggle. Amongst these individuals Marx, whose opponents even—those of them who were intellectually honest, at least—have always considered him a thinker of great import, is the victim of an at times conscious, at times unconscious conspiracy of silence. Most texts of social psychology completely ignore his theories, others mention them only in very distorted fashion. But it is daily becoming more obvious that despite certain methodological limitations of the Marxian system, the time is past when social science may ignore Marx. (Pp. 167–169; italics added)

Using a different language and conceptual scheme, Brown is saying essentially the same thing that Dewey said about the political conditioning of the psychologist; that is, the internal and external behavior of the psychologist cannot be understood in narrowly individual terms but has to be seen in terms of where he or she is in the social order. This does not mean, and this is a point that Brown hammers home, that social niche explains everything. But it does mean that if you know the social role and niche of the psychologist, you will be right more often than wrong in predicting how he will describe the social order; how he will explain how it does and ought to change; his theories about how to account for individual differences within and between groups (e.g., the sexes, races, socioeconomic groupings); and, fatefully, what theories and actions would never occur to him or that he would dismiss out of hand.

There can be no greater contrast to Brown's book than E. L. Thorndike's *Human Nature and the Social Order*. Published originally in 1940, the book was republished in abridged form in 1969 with an introduction by G. J. Clifford. For all practical purposes Thorndike accepts the social order in the most uncritical manner. One would never know that this massive collection of data was assembled during the Great Depression, when cataclysmic changes in the international order were also occurring. In fact, after reading the book it would be understandable for one to conclude that our society is a static one unrelated to a complex past and moving smoothly and scientifically into a glorious future. In the introduction to the abridged edition Clifford states: "Economic suffering stood in the foreground of the social malaise that was the Great Depression and that spurred Thorndike and the Carnegie Corporation to undertake the project" (p. xiv). Unlike Brown, who saw the Great Depression (and earlier ones in our society) as standing in some intimate relationship to the features of a capitalist society, here and in other Western countries, Thorndike's approach is ahistorical and superficial in the extreme. Clifford goes on to say that Thorndike was far more interested in "*individual* behavior" (italics Clifford) than in "*social* institutions" (italics Clifford). Clifford then quotes approvingly (p. xv) a review of Thorndike's book by a professor of sociology at the University of London and the London School of Economics:

> Something must be said, however, on the adequacy of the general theory of human nature and society which is here adopted as the basis of inquiry. We must ask, to begin with, whether a theory of society can be built upon the basis of a psychology of individual differences. Prof. Thorndike seems to think that the differences between communities resolve themselves ultimately into differences in endowment of the individuals composing them or in the range of the distribution. But social structure can scarcely be interpreted in these terms . . . social classes . . . , for example, are not in the main determined by differences in individual endowment, and changes from one type of stratification to another have nothing to do with changes in genetic endowment. Similarly, on the basis of very similar genetic endowment very different social institutions can be built up. A science of society must therefore be largely a study of social forces, that is, of the forces which arise out of the relations between human beings. . . . *Psychology cannot do the work of sociology.* (P. xv)

Given the substance of Clifford's introduction, one wonders why the book, even in abridged form, was republished. Thorndike certainly deserves high praise for trying to integrate psychology with other social sciences for the purpose of understanding the social order better. Compared to other eminent mainstream psychologists of his times Thorndike at least tried to see things whole. If his effort was sadly and fatally flawed, if his effort revealed how much Thorndike was a prisoner of his own socialization, if his effort illustrated the limitations of a psychology of individuals, if Thorndike's book (unlike Brown's) has to be viewed today as obsolete, Thorndike nevertheless was grappling with a complex issue that psychology today has yet to address.

I am reminded here of a meeting in our department many years ago. For reasons I do not remember we found ourselves discussing how a university could avoid having a lot of tenured deadwood. A colleague, Frank Beach, came up (half facetiously) with the plan that when a person was hired at the instructor level, he would be given tenure but that as he sought promotion to higher levels there would be less tenure, and at the associate and professor levels there would be no tenure. Everyone laughed and the discussion went in new directions. The reaction to Beach's proposal was in no way consciously self-serving; the speed of dismissal was too quick to say that anyone reflected on it. But in all respects that reaction illustrated how successfully socialized we were into a role and niche that was embedded in an institutional structure we considered right, that defined how we would perceive ourselves and others in that structure, that determined the basis for movement and decisionmaking in the hierarchy, that influenced how we would understand and judge those who did not make it, and that contributed to how we would view those who were outside the structure. In short, how we viewed tenure reflected a very complex array of interrelated perceptions, attitudes, and values that said, so to speak, "This is the way our world is and ought to be." But we did not have to say that or even be aware of what such a statement stood for. *That* was our world and that was the way it should be. We considered ourselves reasonable people whose view of tenure was uninfluenced by our socialization or by a reluctance to entertain new ideas suggesting an alteration in the distribution of power, perquisites, and an orientation toward the future. We knew we were a prestigious department in a prestigious university, a bastion of excellence upholding standards and traditions ever under attack from various quarters! We were in a special and privileged position in the society and what was good for us was good for society; what society sometimes considered good for it was not always good for us.

I chose this example to illustrate two facts of general import. First, the socialization process whereby we come to occupy a role and social niche is ordinarily so effective that we are unaware of the degree to which that process has shaped our thinking, actions, and world view. Second, the extent that we are unaware of the nature and effectiveness of the process we cannot begin to control for the sources of bias inherent in that (or any other) sustained socialization process. Put in another way, we attribute to our thinking (including theories) and actions an unwarranted degree of objectivity, self-determination, and rationality. In some abstract, isolated sense we know that we are products of a particular, complicated socialization process but in the concrete (e.g., tenure) we act as though our thinking and behavior were independent of the world view that powers that process. Examine the psychological theories of man in society and you will be very hard put to find any evidence that the theorist explicitly has confronted the relationship between the substance of his or her theory and the social role and niche the theorist occupies. Theory is presented as though it were completely independent of the influences of time, place, social role, and niche. Here, too, there is the irony that the historically minded psychological theorist of man in society knows that the substance of the theories of his or her predecessors was obviously and powerfully influenced by who and where they were in their society although they were unaware of these influences. That is to say, among other shortcomings (e.g., faulty observations, personal blind spots, lack of rigor or system) that the passage of time may have exposed, it is now obvious that no less interfering than these shortcomings were who and where the predecessors were in the society of their time, i.e., the nature of the world view that undergirded the socialization process that led them to occupy the social role and niche they did. Today's psychological theorists may know this to be true for their predecessors but give no evidence that they are grappling with such a problem themselves.*

There were other purposes to my choice of the tenure anecdote.

---

*This is the case in other fields as well. So, for example, Isaac Newton is regarded as one of the supreme scientists of all time: the epitome of the rational, systematic experimentalist, mathematician, physicist, and theoretician. We forget that for Newton God was an indispensable factor in his cosmology (Koyre, 1965). Similarly, for the Pythagoreans numbers were not just numbers: each had symbolic meanings that today we regard as fanciful and strange in the extreme. But in so regarding them we gloss over the fact that our world view is in unexamined ways as distorting an influence on our thinking as the world views of the Pythagoreans and Newton were on their way of thinking.

That anecdote is dated in that it refers to a time when most psychologists worked in colleges and universities, a fact that exerted an enormous influence on the substance of the field although that influence, as I have emphasized, went unexamined. Beginning around 1950, and as a direct result of World War II, increasing numbers of psychologists sought work outside the university. It is consistent with my argument that academic psychology had no theoretical-conceptual basis for recognizing that this shift in work site potentially represented a variety of challenges and threats to the status and influence of academic psychology. It was not only a matter of the number of psychologists who would be outside the university; more important was the fact that precisely because they would be in new roles and niches in settings differing widely in tradition, structure, and ambience from those of the university they would develop their own view of what psychology is or should be. There was absolutely nothing in psychological theory that would allow these developments to be formulated. To be sure, there were academic psychologists who were opposed to these developments but the opposition was based not on a formal psychology but rather on simple, vague beliefs about what would contribute to progress in psychology. That this future progress bore an amazing resemblance to their view of progress in the past escaped attention and analysis. It could hardly be otherwise because whatever psychology they had was about asocial individuals and their minds, not about the relationships between thinking and behavior, on the one hand, and socialization into social role and niche, on the other. They did not possess a psychology that made them self-conscious about how their embeddedness in and commitment to a societal institution could have both negative and positive effects, could be liberating as well as imprisoning.

Today, academic psychologists are a minority in the American Psychological Association and, as one might have expected, this change has been accompanied by sharp conflicts about who is a psychologist, the structure and substance of graduate education, where psychology is or ought to be going, and the degree to which (if at all) departments of psychology should be responsive to the changing needs of society as those needs are perceived by the thousands of psychologists outside the university. And there is still another conflict around the proposal that departments of psychology be accredited by an independent national body. It is beyond my present purpose to examine in detail the rhetoric and merits of the different positions in the controversies. *What is relevant for my purpose is that academic psychologists now see their nonacademic colleagues from a perspective from which they have been unable to see themselves.* That is to say, they see nonacademic psychologists as a group occupying roles and niches justified in self-serving ways albeit formulated in terms of the public welfare. The nonacademic psychologists, of course, see academic psychologists in the same way. The two groups are becoming more polarized, both secure in the feeling that they are defending impersonal, objective truths. Both groups agree that each works in a different world and that this has determined how each sees its own world and those of others. Neither group, however, is able to recognize the possibility that what they agree about must be a source of bias not only in their view of the world but also in their differing views about the substance of psychology. It is one thing to recognize the obvious fact that where you are in the social order mightily influences what and how you think; it is quite another to recognize that these influences always introduce distortions of a self-serving nature stemming from socialization into roles and niches.

It is relevant here to add the concluding sentence I omitted from an earlier quotation from J. F. Brown (1936). The italics are his: *"Marx is undoubtedly the most important social psychologist of modern times on the question of the effect of social class membership on the social psychology of the individual, when the class struggle exists."* The concept of class struggle has an antique, even offensive, sound to our ears. This was true even in 1936, when Brown's book was published. That response is typically American (the United States), contradicting as the concept does every aspect of our national rhetoric and ideology. In the thirties that concept was already a rallying point for peoples in Europe (e.g., Spain, Italy, Germany), and in the post–World War II era it has served the same function for the peoples of Africa and Asia. What we in this country have failed to understand—less excusable among social scientists than among other groups—is that our socialization gives us a view of ourselves and the world that ill prepares us to view ourselves in relation to the world. Social scientists were totally unprepared, even in broad outline, for the transformations of the modern world.

What is at issue here is not the validity of the concept of the class struggle in Marxist theory, because that can be questioned on many grounds, but rather our inability to understand that people in other countries perceive and act on a concept of social class in ways quite different from ours. We cannot understand their "psychology" because our own psychology fails to make us self-conscious about its derivation from our society and about its relationship to where psychologists are in that society. We believed, naively, that we had or were developing a general psychology free of social bias, i.e., a psychology of man (any man) in society (any society). *As a result, we saw, understood, and reacted to people in other societies from the same distorted perspective that determined how we would see, understand, and react to every immigrant group that has ever entered our society.* These pages in the history, past and present, of psychology and the other social sciences are not pleasant reading. They contain a lesson that may well be Marx's most enduring contribution, one that is the basis for Brown's judgment that Marx is the most significant social psychologist of modern times. It is a deceptively simple conceptualization: the nature of a person's work and the place of that work in the social order are the most significant shapers of the substance, structure, and scope of the person's consciousness!

Ironically, this view has gained some acceptance among social scientists. For example, in their introduction to a book of readings, *Class, Status, and Power* (1953), Bendix and Lipset state: *"All these investigations assume, more or less explicitly, that the social and economic position of the individual determines his ideas and actions, if not completely, then 'by and large,' and if not now, then 'in the long run' "* (p. 13; italics added). What is ironic is that social scientists have managed to avoid applying this conceptualization to themselves. This avoidance has been far stronger in psychology because it has for so long been preoccupied with individuals, not individuals in a social-economic-vocational context that is enmeshed in a larger social matrix. Psychologists, of course, recognize social class as a "variable" and employ measures of it, but in the process of "objectifying" it they rob it of its significance. For example, of the few social scientists who have truly illuminated the psychological significance of social class in certain parts of our society, no one has made a greater contribution than Lloyd Warner in his Yankee City studies (1964). But following these pioneer studies Warner and others developed shorthand indices of social class position. The number of studies by psychologists using these indices must run into the thousands. Unfortunately, one has to conclude that few psychologists read Warner's earlier studies, otherwise they would have noticed that *their* use of a numerical index does not refer to the meanings and consequences of social class in the lives of Yankee City citizens. I would argue that the use of a social class index (e.g., based on income, education, occupation) has obscured more than it has clarified the psychological significance of the concept in people's lives in this society.

What is at issue is not that by virtue of many selective factors psychologists as a group have important niches and roles in the social order. Nor am I making the equally obvious point that the socialization process by which psychologists become what they are affects them as people any less than it does those in other groups in similar or different socioeconomic strata. The important issue arises from the fact that psychologists develop theories of human behavior that they take seriously or want others to take seriously, and seriously means that they and/or others will act to influence the lives of people. What I am contending is that those theories and actions cannot be assumed to be independent of who in the social order can become a psychologist, of the socialization process whereby one obtains credentials as a psychologist, and of the status and influence society gives to psychologists.

The substance of any psychological theory has many sources and one of the most important, albeit unrecognized, sources is where the psychologist is in the social order. Earlier I illustrated this point by briefly discussing how psychologists used their theories in relation to immigrant groups, unaware of the possibility that by conforming to the outlook of others in their social stratum they were exposing how successfully socialized they had been into those stratum. Of course, they were not conforming in any conscious sense. There was no need for that because they could see no conflict between the substance of their theories and implied actions, on the one hand, and what was good for their society, on the other. Their theories, they assumed, were uncontaminated by who and where they were in their society. The history of psychological theories, from the Greeks to the present day, completely refutes that assumption. And yet that assumption continues to be made. This should occasion no surprise because to question that assumption is truly upsetting: it is no less upsetting (perhaps more) than feeling yourself driven by forces that you do not understand or cannot identify. Your "theory" of who you are and how you became what you are is no longer working. You dimly sense that what is called for is a redefinition of your past in relation to the social world. Most of us shrink from pursuing the task, muddling through life wanting to change but managing not to.

Freud's self-analysis is regarded as a major chapter in the history of human courage. I intend no derogation of that assessment when I note two adverse consequences of what he did. First, it mightily reinforced the focus on the individual born into and reared in a certain kind of family, a focus that ignored society. Second, in making public his findings and theory in the form he did, Freud reinforced the fiction that their substance stood in no relationship either to his society or to his place in society. If you read the corpus of Freud's writings you would be extremely hard put to figure out, even in broad outline, what his society was like.* And you would be equally hard put to figure out Freud's relationship to that society, especially in regard to how much of that society was in him. That relationship, Freud and his biographers tell us, bore the stamp of the fact that Freud was Jewish, but they do not emphasize the significance of the strength of Freud's wish to be recognized in the *traditional* ways of his society. It is not a contradiction to note that in conformity with the scientific zeitgeist Freud did not want his theories to be perceived as bounded by time and place (and even culture) but rather as universally true for the past and present.

Freud was too well socialized (as a person, psychologist, physician, and physiologist) to be disposed to use his self-analysis as a way of exploring how and to what degree the society was in him. Take, for example, Freud's response to a paper, contained in the discussions of the Vienna Psychoanalytic Society in 1910. The topic was *On Suicide: With Particular Reference to Suicide among Young Students.* (Freud, S., quoted in Friedman, 1967)

> You have all listened with much satisfaction to the plea put forward by an educationalist who will not allow an unjustified charge to be levelled against the institution that is so dear to him. But I know that in any case you were not inclined to give easy credence to the accusation that schools drive their pupils to suicide. Do not let us be carried too far, however, by

---

*Freud recognized that there are classes of very unequal power in society and that their relationships to each other are crucial and can change in ways that are dangerous to the society. Beyond that, however, Freud manifested little interest in the nature of the social order, where he saw himself in that order, and how his place in it may have been reflected in the substance of his theorizing. Similarly, although Freud obviously knew he was both male and a father, he could not pursue how those facts entered into his theorizing. As Schafer (1973) points out in his effort to recast the language of psychoanalytic theory (and inevitably its substance): "Almost always Freud presented the analytic relationship in terms of the relationship with the father." Dollard (1935), in his unfortunately neglected *Criteria for the Life History,* gives many examples of Freud's narrow focus on the asocial individual. It needs also to be noted that early on Dollard clearly pointed out how misdirected psychology was in its study of the asocial individual.

our sympathy with the party which has been unjustly treated in this instance. Not all the arguments put forward by the opener of the discussion seem to me to hold water. If it is the case that youthful suicide occurs not only among pupils in secondary schools but also among apprentices and others, this fact does not acquit the secondary schools; it must perhaps be interpreted as meaning that as regards its pupils the secondary school takes the place of the traumas with which other adolescents meet in other walks of life. But a secondary school should achieve more than not driving its pupils to suicide. It should give them a desire to live and should offer them support and backing at a time of life at which the conditions of their development compel them to relax their ties with their parental home and their family. It seems to me indisputable that schools fail in this, and in many respects fall short of their duty of providing a substitute for the family and of arousing interest in life in the world outside. This is not a suitable occasion for a criticism of secondary schools in their present shape; but perhaps I may emphasize a single point. The school must never forget that it has to deal with immature individuals who cannot be denied a right to linger at certain stages of development and even at certain disagreeable ones. The school must not take on itself the inexorable character of life: it must not seek to be more than a *game* of life. (P. 60)

There is much in what Freud states that illustrates my point but I shall restrict my comments to certain of his remarks. What does Freud mean by the "conditions of their development compel them to relax their ties with their parental home and family"? Clearly, Freud is referring to forces within the individual, forces that arise and get played out in the context of family and home. Freud is not interested in why family characteristics lead the young person to feel compelled "to relax his ties" with it. For Freud the characteristics are all narrowly psychological and intra- and inter-personal, and he cannot entertain the possibility that these characteristics stand in some relationship to the traditions of the society and to the social–economic–political–vocational basis on which that society is organized. Note that Freud wants the schools to arouse in pupils "interest in life in the world outside," the implication being that this goal is not one that the family is organized to do well. Why this division of function which, if it exists to any degree, cannot be explained only in psychological terms? Note further that because of their immaturity Freud wants secondary school pupils to be protected from the "inexorable character of life." That the degree of immaturity Freud perceives may be unjustified or that the immaturity is as much a consequence of the way the society is organized and affects family life as it is a feature of individual psychological development, are possibilities that cannot occur to Freud. There is the individual, the family, the school, and *then* life! And what is there about "life" that students should be shielded from? Freud has a view of his society that he assumes is shared by all others in his society. And if he does not make that unwarranted assumption, how does he account for differing perceptions? And that is the point: Freud sees his society from the vantage point of his role and niche in it and he cannot confront the implications of the bias that such a vantage point may introduce. Almost at the same time that Freud was recommending that school have the features of a *game* (italics Freud's), John Dewey was saying that school is not a preparation for life but life itself. The difference between these contradictory views is largely a function of the fact that Dewey, far more than Freud, saw schools embedded in a structured and stratified society which, willy-nilly, impacted on schools and their inhabitants, and that if students, particularly the less socially advantaged ones, were to deal effectively with society, the artificiality of the distinction between school and life had to be exposed and eliminated. Amongst many things, Dewey was a student of his society and if (like Freud) he did not like what he saw in that society, he did not see games as a way of dealing with it. Dewey was far ahead of his contemporaries in psychology in seeing that the place of people (psychologists and those they studied) in the social order was potent in determining their outlook and opportunities. Why Dewey was able to liberate himself from the confines of his social role deserves more study than it has received. It is not fortuitous that J. F. Brown was very knowledgeable about Dewey.

Let us turn to more current examples. Why is it that only in the last two decades psychologists have come to see that their theories about human development and behavior had little to say about women, and most of that was seriously biased? (The same question can be asked in relation to various minorities, the mentally ill, and the mentally handicapped.) If psychologists have changed their views, it is because they have been forced (I use that word advisedly) to recognize that most psychologists have been men, for the most part studying males, members of marriages in which there was an economic and social division of labor supported in diverse ways by incentives and sanctions. You could say that psychologists as a group were not distinctive in this respect, i.e., most males shared similar views. But that is avoiding the point that psychologists were no better than other male groups in overcoming their socialization, and it underlines the point that in their quest for sources of bias in theories, research, and social practice psychologists were amazingly insensitive to bias by virtue of gender, social role, and niche. If psychologists are more sensitive today it is because their eyes have been opened to aspects of how our society is structured. It would be wrong to say that psychologists have learned something about women; it would be more correct to say that they have learned something about their *society,* and their role in it, they did not know before. That may be too optimistic a conclusion because some psychologists seem far more comfortable talking about women in the abstract than women in the past and present web of society. They talk about or perceive a women's revolution as though the sources and consequences of a societal revolution could be comprehended in narrow psychological terms. If in C. Wright Mills's term psychologists lack the "sociological imagination" (as he felt most social scientists did) and resort to "psychologisms" for understanding complex social phenomena, it says a good deal about how little psychologists understand their socialization.

Mills was one of the few post–World War II social scientists who recognized how unreflective his colleagues were about how their place in the social order was an influence both on their theories and on their willing role as agents for maintaining the status quo. He became increasingly and stridently critical of our social order, of its impact internationally, and of the inability of social scientists to face up to the more seamy effects of our society on its citizens and people in emerging nations. A similar view and transformation will be discussed later in this chapter when I take up Gladwin's (1980) *Slaves of the White Myth: The Psychology of Neocolonialism.*

I have deliberately refrained from using with precision such terms as social role, niche, social structure, social class, and stratification because they are abstractions that do not convey how the substance and direction of socialization come to have several effects—shaping our perceptions and conceptions of how the society is organized; influencing how we explain why the different groups in society are what they are; determining in large part how we view social change and participate in social action; and limiting our awareness about how much of the larger society and of the particular segment into which we were born and have developed is in us. When I encounter these abstractions in the literature I am reminded of patients in psychotherapy who know and use psychological jargon in ways that effectively protect them from talking concretely about what they think and feel. They are adept at labeling themselves at the expense of self-scrutiny. Unfortunately, there are many psychotherapists who, like many social scientists, employ the same abstractions when they talk to or describe others. I am in no way suggesting that such terms as social class, social role, and niche are inappropriate or invalid but rather that for my purposes they obscure as much as they reveal.

What I mean may become clearer when I say that the major points I have been at pains to make have been best described and elaborated by novelists. Henry James, Edith Wharton, J. P. Marquand, J. G. Couzzens, Thomas Wolfe, William Faulkner, Joyce Carol Oates, James Farrell, Louis Auchincloss, Edwin O'Connor, John O'Hara—this is a small sample of American novelists in whose writings we come to know individuals in terms of time, place, tradition, and culture. We come to know these individuals, we are fascinated by them, not because they are intrinsically interesting as single individuals but because of the writers' artistry in helping us understand how the individual, on the one hand, and time and the social historical characteristics of place, on the other, are inextricably part of each other. In our daily lives we tend to lose the sense of place, its physical characteristics and their impact on us, and how the larger physical surround shapes our thinking, actions, and outlook. We are not used to examining dispassionately our physical ecology unless some event jolts us into recognizing what we have been taking for granted or what we did not want to think about. It is then that our sense of embeddedness in our physical surround undergoes change. What is true for physical surround is no less true for our social surround, and what the novelists do so well is to make us understand what the central characters in the story do not understand: there is a structure to their social world that they never comprehend, a structure that in turn reflects the characteristics of a larger social arena. In some novels there is that moment of truth when the individual becomes aware how incomplete his or her understanding was of the world. Not only does the individual now see other people differently but also the basis for understanding relationships among people undergoes change. And so the individual comes to view the moment of truth as the ending of an age of innocence during which he or she falsely believed that the locus of control was firmly in the self, a fiction nurtured by traditions and a socialization process that identified what is with what should be and explicit rhetoric with implicit ideology.

One of the major contributions of modern experimental social psychology has been the demonstration (somewhat ad nauseum) that an individual's behavior is determined in part by situational factors of which he or she is unaware. Individuals explain their behavior in terms of processes within themselves, whereas the findings from experimental manipulations clearly implicate external factors. Indeed, these findings are so robust that they have presented serious problems for personality theorists who seek to explain behavior in terms of traits relatively stable from situation to situation. The ingenuity of experimental social psychologists has far outstripped either their thoughtfulness or their curiosity. On the one hand, they endlessly demonstrate that it is possible so to structure an individual's here and now environment that it will impact upon him or her even though the individual will not perceive the sources of impact. On the other, the respect experimental social psychologists have for the principle being demonstrated seems to hold only for the type of situation their imagination and resources permit. It seems never to have occurred to them to ask: "If I assume, as I must, that what is true for my experimental subjects is in principle true for me, what are the possible sources of impact on me and my theories that I am not aware of? Have I been assuming that I know the major sources of *my* behavior and *my* theories?" Such issues, however, cannot arise as long as the social psychologist focuses on the types of situations he or she contrives to structure and does not pursue the implications of the general principle he or she is demonstrating. One of the obstacles is the very concept of situational factors, which in practice reduce to transient interpersonal perceptions. Precisely because they are transient, attention is diverted from applying the principle to social contexts into which every one of us is born and develops, contexts in which the principle is so well illustrated by novelists.

Social psychologists are not a random sample of the population, an obvious fact not taken seriously by them despite their exquisite sensitivity to the mischief that nonrandomness works in the interpretation of ideas and research findings. By virtue of length and type of education, income, site of work, professional identifications, social status and prestige, tools of the trade, and commitment to certain rites of passage, psychologists occupy a distinct niche in society. Like the people they study in the situations they contrive, social psychologists live as citizens and professionals in a structured milieu. Unlike the situations they contrive the milieu is not of their making and has a long social-institutional history that implicates far more than the milieu itself. The milieu is grounded in history and so is the social psychologist, and these are grounds enough, warning enough, to conclude that his or her theories about human behavior reflect influences of which the social psychologist is unaware. The question is not whether this is true or even the ways in which it may be true, but rather why this has been so true among social psychologists (although by no means peculiar to them)? It is to restate and not to answer the question to ask: unlike the novelists I mentioned, who so artfully have illuminated how individuals are unaware of the ways in which the fabric and structure of their conscious being and interpersonal relationships are determined by the structure of their milieu, why have social psychologists been unable to apply the principle to themselves and their field? This is not an argumentum ad hominem. It is not a question of motivation. It is a question of the environment or social ecology of theories about human behavior. We require that theorists tell us how they came by their theories, but to accept their accounts as explanations is to deny either the validity or the general applicability of a principle that social psychologists have again and again demonstrated in their experiments. In demonstrating the principle the social psychologist is, so to speak, hoisted by his or her own petard: what in the ground from which my theory as figure emerged am I unaware of?

If we look to the novelists I listed, we begin to see the first step to an answer. In all cases their novels are about milieus and their inhabitants the writer knows well—they are milieus into which the writer was born and reared or with which he or she has had sustained contact. But these are not autobiographical novels. What makes these novels so important as social descriptions and so illuminating of individual lives is the ability and courage of the literary artists to transcend their embeddedness in the milieu, to take distance from themselves at the same time that they use themselves, all for two related purposes: to distinguish between the milieu as it is and the milieu as the individual perceives it and to show how much of the former is unknown to but influential on the individual. These novelists have deliberately tried to transcend their milieus—to comprehend the milieu in its terms, to say it like it is and not the way you want it to be or the way you were told it should be. These novelists do not aim to be factual in a journalistic sense, or to convey a picture, snapshot style, but rather to weave a social texture that is far more understandable to *us* than it ever is to the major characters. We, the readers, know more than the central characters do because the novelist has been our teacher, and the best teachers are those who, having broken out of the confines of their past, warn us about how to stay out of prisons. The most important message they give us is that because there is more to this world than our conscious explanations take account of (the principle the social psychologist demonstrates) we must hold our explanations suspect, especially those that describe our embeddedness in the social world, i.e., our explanations of our own psychology.

It is relevant but far beyond the boundaries of my knowledge to determine why some novelists understand and convey so well the principle that each of us constantly breathes in our social surround as effortlessly and unreflectively as we breathe in air. It is only when the composition of that air changes or when certain bodily alterations occur that we become aware that there is a structure to the inside and outside previously unexamined. Similarly, I suspect, the novelists I have referred to experienced some long-standing inside-outside conflict that led them to take distance both from their milieu and from themselves. (Both Edith Wharton and Henry James spent most of their mature years in foreign lands.) The conflicts were neither interpersonal nor intrapersonal. Indeed, the concept of conflict may be inappropriate or misleading (not, however, in the cases of Wharton and James) for my purposes because it diverts attention away from the more important fact that, whatever the reasons, these novelists came to understand that the workings of the individual mind and workings of the social surroundings are part of a larger picture. And that larger picture had structure and character explainable only in social historical terms. The religious, political, economic, physical, demographic, geneological—these are the parts that make up the larger picture much of which the individual cannot see but much of which shapes his being. And therein lies our debt to these novelists: they help us ''see'' what is influential but not seeable. Just as the ingenuity of the experimental social psychologist inheres in the demonstration that the explanations by individuals of their behavior do not implicate significant characteristics of the experimental situation, the artistry of the novelist inheres in the same demonstration of the principle but in regard to an arena of society that is infinitely more complicated as well as more directly meaningful to us. This the novelist could not do, certainly not do well, without first working the principle through, to some extent at least, in regard to his or her social arena. This working through has been avoided by the psychologist. Writing a novel, like crafting a theory or devising an experiment, requires a point of view. Unlike the psychologist, the novelist's point of view is quite consciously forged from a self-examination. But that is only a beginning that is followed by the equally (or more) difficult task of using that self-examination to project dispassionately, creatively, and compellingly, a story that stands on its own. Indeed, the best novels are those in which we are never aware of how the novelist is influencing us.

Let us turn to a recent book that is remarkable on three counts. First, it illustrates in the most detailed, compelling, and provoking way the central points I have tried to make in this and previous chapters. Second, it is in part a saga of how an anthropologist came to see and overcome the dimensions of his confinement within his discipline and his society. Third, the book is about a set of issues and processes that have direct relevance to every person on this earth. The book, by Thomas Gladwin (1980), is *Slaves of the White Myth: The Psychology of Neocolonialism*. Gladwin starts from a particular premise:

This book starts from the premise of the Third World authors that the most devastating impact of the white man was psychological, with the exercise of force secondary. It undertakes to examine the nature and trace the history of this subversive process. Almost at once it becomes clear that psychological subversion did not have its beginnings only in the years surrounding political independence. Indeed the transformation then of colonialism into equally exploitive neocolonialism was no more than the inevitable fruition of historical forces set in motion with the very first intrusion of white men into the lands they were later to colonize so easily.

It is equally clear that it was not the color of the white man's skin nor any other inherited physical or psychological characteristic which accounted for his influence. His power lay instead in what he brought with him, not in himself. Guns come to mind, but at the outset they were rarely used. The white man's conquest was not primarily a military operation. The major battles which did take place came later, between the white men and natives who were revolting against an already established white presence. What the white man brought instead was a completely new set of values, a system which was social and economic, but which was even more fundamentally psychological. It was so devastating because it contained its own driving force; once the system had been introduced by the newcomers, the natives soon found themselves unable to avoid living also by its rules and values, and then imposing them upon their fellows.

This system has come to be known as capitalism. Having evolved originally in Europe, capitalism had already put its mark upon the minds of the very first white men known to have come to the Third World. Almost all white men, even those who oppose the capitalist system and its exploitation of the poor by the rich, have taken for granted the universality of capitalist values: that all human beings are at heart individualistic, and all are motivated ultimately by their own self-interest. Indeed, it is commonplace by now to accept these qualities as at the core of "human nature," and therefore inescapable.

Yet before the white men came, most of the people of the non-white world did not live by these values. Their lives and their transactions were instead guided by the moral obligations of kinship and mutual interdependence. It was a way of life which offered no rewards to the nonconformist bent on pursuing his own self-interest. Instead, individual selfishness had to be dealt with severely because theirs was a system which depended upon the unquestioning cooperation of everyone in order to meet equally the needs of all. This dependence on universal cooperation turned out to be the Achilles' heel of what is now the Third World. When the white man came, with his values shaped by capitalist society, he naturally approached the people he met as individuals responsible only to themselves. It was the only way he knew. Whether he sought their help or demanded it, he treated people as individuals. He usually gave them something in return for what he wanted from them, compensating each for his own separate labor, or perhaps punishing a few for their individual "laziness." This was a dramatically new way for people to relate to one another. With the exception of slaves, the harder a person worked the more benefits he was likely to receive from these new white men. In other words, self-interest began to carry its own rewards, and individual effort became a feasible alternative to dependence upon the web of kin obligations. The formerly durable fabric of traditional life, once it had begun to be weakened by the taint of self-interest, was soon ripped to shreds. The old values spread outward to take their place almost before anyone realized what was happening. (Pp. 258–259)

Capitalism, Gladwin is saying, has at its root a conception of man as an individual "naturally" motivated by self-interest and the desire for material possession and gain. Every form of societal organization, past or present, rests on a conception of the individual but not every form has the potent thrust of capitalism to regard and therefore to shape the individual as self-contained and self-enhancing.

> The most profoundly destructive effect of capitalism on a communal, kinship-oriented society lay in undermining the bonds of family, clan, and community. The competition and individualism which is a necessary part of capitalism isolated people and family units from one another, diluting their responsibility toward the people among whom they were born, and in turn destroying the security of being able to count on their own family for help. The problems of money, going into debt, having to buy things one needs from wages which are too small, cheating, stealing, bribery, and corruption, as well as many other painful difficulties of a money economy are also a part of capitalist existence. But in comparison to the breaking of those familiar ties which traditionally bound people to one another and guaranteed mutual cooperation and support, the harassments of living in a world of money must be considered secondary. People can learn to deal with the problems of money and private property, but once the bonds of kinship are weakened they can never be fully restored.
>
> The extended family was, before the white man came, far more than a means of linking people into a cooperative work force and a source of mutual support in time of need. It was an educational institution, often placing children in the care of their grandparents, who were rich in the knowledge and wisdom of maturity. It was a judicial system in which elders, who knew everyone intimately, resolved grievances and disputes in preference to meting out harsh punishments. It was a forerunner of psychiatry, giving comfort, advice, sympathy and tolerance to people who were troubled. Through ceremony and tradition it linked people to the forces of nature upon which their existence depended. The extended family thus fulfilled the basic needs—material, psychological, and spiritual—of every person within it. True, members had to conform to the customs and obligations of the group and submit to the decisions of their elders. Sometimes this was a heavy burden, but in return, the group of kinsmen offered the support of many hands and the security of a common identity. This did not necessarily assure tranquility, but it did render the hazards of daily existence controllable. But when the new ways undermined the extended family and finally brought about its collapse, every individual was forced to face problems alone in a world he only half understood. (Pp. 260–261)

Why, Gladwin asks, did people so readily and consistently choose to break away and to enter an alien system full of uncertainties and, all to often, miseries?

But why were their warnings so readily dismissed? Could not everyone see the truth of the warnings all about them? To us, accustomed to change and adept at recognizing its first signs, this would have been natural; we would have seen more clearly the chaos which lay ahead. But one of the virtues of traditional societies was their stability. They did change, but slowly and by consensus gradually arrived at. Sudden dramatic upheavals in their lives rarely took place, so they had little experience in anticipating or adapting to them. Here and there, grave intrusions did occur and their results were usually catastrophic. Vast empires were created, before the white man came, in Mexico, South America, Central and West Africa, and Asia. The conquerers were resisted, often bitterly, but once defeat came, it was usually easy to convert conquered peoples to vassals of the empire. In a sense their collapse then was analogous to the later crumbling of resistance to the white man's system. But there were differences. One was that whereas the ancient empires appeared here and there, the white man soon was everywhere. And in contrast to the sudden and disabling disaster of conquest, the onset of individualistic capitalism was at first slower and more subtle, with its consequences not yet fully obvious even to those who saw many of its dangers.

Its subtlety derived at least in part from the unprecedented nature of the change which was taking place. The military conquests were often brutal, but when they were accomplished they usually did not impose new meanings on the lives of the subjugated, aside from subjugation itself. But the story of the white man's conquest is a story of far more profound conflict, one between two totally contradictory values. It is a conflict which has become almost universal, but as it has been repeated over and again, it has always been unprecedented in each new setting, finding people unprepared to perceive its true dimensions. It is an unequal struggle which has tormented people by the millions, striking at the heart of every society the white man has touched. The two values are simply stated. The traditional value holds that all people are members of a collective groups bound together by a moral obligation to help one another and to work always for the good of the whole. This is sometimes called the moral incentive for work. The white man's morality, derived from the capitalist ethic, declares that all men are free, responsible only for themselves, and free to compete, exploit one another, and work for their own personal gain. This is the material incentive for work. Of course much more than work incentives is involved, including the nature and philosophy of a society, and the way each person sees himself in relation to the rest of the world. But it is useful to retain the idea of incentives for work because the material incentive, and the pursuit of self-interest which it implies, was the cutting edge of capitalism, and the white man's most

powerful psychological weapon in subduing the Third World. (Pp.
261–262)

Gladwin has not written a polemic. Nor is he posing the problem
in terms of good and bad people or between earlier Edens and current
hells. We are never left in doubt that Gladwin believes that in the process of dominating and controlling the Third World capitalism essentially destroyed the communal basis of living, unwittingly contributing
over time to a situation in which what it destroyed in others it now
poignantly but fruitlessly seeks for itself. How did this come about? A
large part of the answer, and one that Gladwin documents in detail, is
that those who operated in the capitalist framework of thinking were so
unquestioning of their moral and intellectual superiority, so convinced
that there were no alternative world views they might consider, that
they had no qualms about what they were doing to others. It was not a
matter of failing to understand (or trying to understand) peoples who
were different. The fact is that the colonizers believed they understood
well what these peoples were and why it was so important to change
them. What they thought they understood was perversely a reflection
of how the colonizers explained themselves to themsleves; that is, they
saw the native as an individual possessed of motives that resided in
him or her and the goal of which was self-enhancement. They could
not see, nor were they disposed to ''see,'' communal-family structure,
history, and tradition. And if they were not so disposed it was because
they did not understand how successfully socialized they themselves
had been to a particular world view in which the ''free'' individual is
preeminent. To be disposed to understand other people in their social-
historical context, and to do this with a semblance of dispassion, requires not only that you have attempted to do this for yourself in your
context but also that you have become sensitive to the dangers and difficulties such a task engenders. But, as Gladwin emphasizes, the colonizers were set to control, not to understand.

Gladwin's book is clearly written but not easy reading. He is not
content to recount past history but rather goes on to show how the
more things change the more they remain the same. He brings the
story down to the present day and describes the tragic situation in
which the oppressor and the oppressed, no longer seeing themselves in
these terms, nevertheless continue to manifest, albeit subtly, the worst
consequences of their past relationships. Gladwin's book will not be

read by many social scientists, especially his critique of each social science. It is not mainstream psychology; besides, how many psychologists see neocolonialism as a basic issue in or challenge to contemporary psychology? And yet, Gladwin is raising a question that earlier in this century was asked by John Dewey and in the thirties was more directly posed by J. F. Brown: in what ways are psychology's conception of man a reflection of the social-historical-political context? And what that question rests on is the insight that precisely because as a person and a professional the psychologist has been socialized in a context—a process that is intended to be as effective as it is continuous—one has to assume that the relationship between conception and context is a problematic one. Put in another way, one's own culture is both ally and adversary: an ally in providing continuity and an adversary in making it so difficult, and often impossible, to examine certain ideas, to challenge certain values, and to transcend one's own context. To erect a psychology without grappling with these ally-adversary features is to court the trivial, which says much about the history and substance of American psychology. But courting the trivial is among the harmless consequences. What Gladwin has exposed is the harm done when one seems totally unaware that one's theories and practices, far from having socially virginal origins, bear the trademark of one's culture.

How come someone like Gladwin has written the book he did? Although for the most part Gladwin stays out of his book, he does at times tell us about his years of research, administration, and consultation in the Third World. And each time he draws from these experiences it is to use himself as an example of the harm and misunderstanding that are consequences of a world view in which the individual is preeminent, material gain is considered to be both natural and good, and progress is the acceptance of this world view by those unfortunate enough to have grown up in a society lacking the capitalist ethos. Gladwin does not indulge in flagellation of himself and his society or in glorification of Third World countries. He writes dispassionately but forcefully.

One does not have to agree with every aspect of his analysis and critique to conclude that the viability of psychology and the other social sciences depends on the centrality they give to several issues that I reiterate in the next chapter.

CHAPTER VIII

A NEW PSYCHOLOGY
NEED BE BORN

THAT WE ARE BORN and socialized into a particular culture of a particular society in a particular era is a fact, one with which we do not have to wrestle until we experience some disjunction, some sense that something is wrong, between how we feel and the characteristics of our accustomed milieu. At such a time a frequent response is to explain the disjunction in terms of our individual characteristics, e.g., we may blame something about ourselves. Another frequent response is to blame something out there, but usually in overly global or narrow terms. These explanations are more often than not spatially, geographically, and socially circumscribed. Phenomenologically, our world (our *significant* world) is small. We know there is a larger society to which our smaller one is related but here again that relation ordinarily receives only superficial analysis. And we know that the larger society is somehow tied in with other societies on this earth. When I use the pronoun "we" I refer to the way the bulk of us experience our days. But social scientists qua social scientists would never say that the above sentences are in any way appropriate to the way they think about and look at their worlds.

The stock-in-trade of social scientists may vary but they have in common the assumption that society is ordered, and the task of each of them is to figure out how the particular problem in which they are interested is both cause and effect of that order. Aside from psychology, the social sciences have shown more than token respect for the fact that there is a social order, and histories center around competing conceptions of what the social order is, how it came to be, and its future course. Such conceptions are absent from psychology as a formal discipline. It is not that psychology has been unaware of these competing conceptions in the sister disciplines but rather that psychology has regarded these conceptions to be based on weak or faulty assumptions about "human nature." The task of psychology is to probe and conceptualize human nature; then and only then can one understand why the social order has come to have the characteristics it has and, no less important, how to build a better social order. After all, the argument runs, the social order encompasses the varieties of ways in which individuals relate to and affect each other, and these ways will never be comprehensible until we understand the springs, potentials, and limits of individual development. This view has been shared to a significant degree by other social scientists, aware as they are that they are not experts of the human mind. Even before psychology came into formal existence a hundred years ago the other nascent social sciences seized avidly on any new, compelling conception of the nature of man. In the modern era it has been psychoanalysis that the social sciences have embraced because of its scope and emphasis. Freud was never in doubt that his psychology was the foundation on which understanding of the social order would have to be based, and he made several systematic efforts to illustrate the power of his psychology to accomplish the task.

Built into psychology, part of its world view, is the polarity man *and* society. Call it a polarity or a dichotomy or even a distinction, it makes it easy for psychology to focus on one and ignore the other, to avoid dealing with the possibility that the distinction is arbitrary and misleading, that it does violence to the fact that from the moment of birth the individual organism is a social organism, that social means embeddedness in patterned relationships that are but a part of an array of such relationships rooted, among other things, in a social history and a distinctive physical environment. How, then, can you rivet on the individual and ignore that of which he is a part, that which is already part of him, that which is both cause and effect? How can you understand the one and ignore the other? For certain purposes that kind of riveting can be justified but only if one is ever on guard to the possibility that what one records may bear little or no relationship to what is experienced in the naturally occurring social matrix. But psychology never has guarded against this possibility precisely because it began with a man and society distinction that made it seem natural to focus on one and ignore the other. And because it began this way psychology could ignore not only the study of the social order but social history as well. For all practical purposes psychology is ahistorical. It has its subject *matter:* the individual, and all else is commentary—interesting, but commentary.

The reader will recall that in the chapter on John Dewey I emphasized his point that as long as custom and tradition prevail, as long as our world view works, there is no need for a new psychology. In the early chapters of this book I discussed why I think many psychologists feel alienated from the field. For them, psychology no longer works. They have come to believe that the customs and traditions of psychology have proved, generally speaking, to be inadequate, a very frail reed on which to depend either for envisioning the future or for dealing with it. The disaffection has barely surfaced in the psychological literature, if only for the obvious reason that no one likes to admit to bankruptcy. Bankruptcy, it should be noted, does not mean that one is without assets but rather that one does not have enough assets to meet obligations. In the case of psychology those obligations were writ large in the two decades after World War II. As a science and a profession it would produce the knowledge and practices that society needed to become better. More than three decades after World War II there is a growing sense among psychologists that their field misdirected itself and the society.

Central to my argument is the belief that for a new psychology to emerge from the current malaise several issues or questions will have to be confronted. First, why was psychology such a willing, cooperative agent of social policy? That question in no way implies that psychology should have adopted an adversarial, uncooperative stance. But the question does suggest that to the extent that a field becomes an agent of social policy, to the extent that its institutional structures and substantive focuses become dependent on social policies, it dilutes its capacity to take distance from and to fathom the omnipresent, unverbalized assumptions that undergird the customs, traditions, and ideology of the society, *an undergirding that drastically limits the universe of alternatives that social policymakers can consider.* No less significant than what a policy includes are the alternatives to it, which cannot surface in the policy process because they would challenge the policymakers' view of the way things are and ought to be, and that, as I have stressed in previous chapters, is no less true for the psychologist than for the policymaker, which is why the red lights should have started to flash when psychologists found themselves willing agents of social policy. Their willingness, indeed their eagerness, to be such agents set the stage for the current disillusionment. The issue is not whether psychologists should participate in the policy arena—be it in relation to research or education—but whether they do so on the basis of the knowledge that the socialization of the policymaker into his or her society and special niche in it drastically constricts the universe of alternatives that will be recognized.

But there was a more egregious mistake that psychology made and it brings us to the second issue that psychology must confront. The mistake was a consequence of a world view that allowed psychologists to believe that they understood the public arena, how it reflects the social order, and how things get done and on what basis. After all, they had lived their lives in this society, they had a good deal of formal education about their society, and they were, indeed, very bright people. They would have described themselves as knowledgeable about their society, far more so than most other citizens. And they had a special asset: they understood people. But there was another ingredient in their world view, an ahistorical stance, that exposed the scope of their ignorance. More specifically, they (like other social scientists) proceeded on the assumption that their capitalist society had finally learned how to avoid recessions and depressions and, therefore, there would be sufficient (indeed, more and more) resources to support the psychological research and practice the society said it needed. And there was still another related ingredient to this assumption: the *international* order would be largely and favorably influenced by the resources, power, and policies of the United States.

As I indicated in chapter 1, the contrast between this optimistic world view and the one of social scientists today is stark. A central issue that psychology must confront is not only why it was so naive about its society but also the implications of that naivete for the substance of theories of human behavior. Those theories are and never have been independent of the theorists' views of man and society. Once psychology takes this question seriously it no longer can avoid examining what the social order is, how it is changing, its social history, and the implicit axioms that not only give direction to that society but without which the society is literally inexplicable. And to-day, many people, including most social scientists when they are thinking in the quiet of the night, find their society and the world inexplicable, a kind of inkblot in which one can perceive myriad details but no pattern. It is, of course, not fortuitous that in the course of this book I quoted extensively from Dewey, J. F. Brown, Veblen, Gladwin, and Nisbet, a small sample of those thinkers who have sought to uncover the axioms that make explicable, if only in part, the world view that gave and gives direction to our society and was inculcated into the psychological structure of its people. Although they are not thinkers whom psychology views as psychologists, their writings (and those of other like them) explain as much, if not more, about the psychology of people (including social scientists!) in our society than past and present mainstream psychological theories have explained.

The third issue psychology must confront, an issue related to the first two, is the place of psychology in the social order. This is the same as if one were to ask: what is the social and institutional niche of the National Association of Manufacturers? That kind of comparison would not sit well with most psychologists. Why? One part of the answer, the psychologists would say, is that the National Association of Manufacturers pursues and protects the ideological and profit-maximizing interests of a relatively small and privileged group in society. That is to say, they put their interests over those of the general public; they have a view of what society is or should be, of what people are and of what makes them happy, of the regulatory and promotional role of government that is blatantly partisan and factually wrong. In short, the association is in a powerful position in this society and seeks to maintain and to increase that power, which is bad for the society because you simply cannot trust its motives and goals. In so characterizing the association psychologists are telling us a good deal about how they see themselves in the social order as individuals, members of university departments or other agencies, as private practitioners and industrial consultants, as members of the American Psychological Association, etc. They downplay either the presence or strength of the motive of economic gain and growth, that is, *they* do not seek, individually or collectively, to increase their profits in order to purchase more of what they consider the good life. They are agents for the general welfare, not for partisan interests. They do not seek, guildlike, to protect their turf from have-nots who are similarly but mistakenly committed to the public welfare. They seek to gain more public influence because what they stand for and propose is in the best interests of all and not because of any self-serving inclinations. Entrepreneurialship, in the pejorative sense, does not exist in the institutions housing psychology as science or profession. What psychology "manufactures" as science and profession are "products" that will make people happier.

I am not suggesting an identity between the National Association of Manufacturers and the institutions of social science. And I have no doubt that had I been writing this chapter before World War II, when social science was miniscule (compared to today) and housed primarily in the university, the analogy would not have occurred to me, not because in principle it would have been unjustified but simply because the potential for the directions that social science later took would not have been discerned by me. The manufacturers' association and the social sciences come from and have very different histories and traditions, and it should be noted that some of the social sciences (not psychology) developed in part as a response to the worst features of capitalist industrialization. I did not use the analogy to suggest that the gulf between rhetoric and practice is the same for the association and for social science. And I recognize that to the extent that social scientists in their education and training absorb the morality of science (to make one's thinking and procedures public, vigorously to pursue new knowledge) there is a difference between the manufacturers' association and the organs and institutions of social science. I employed the analogy in order to indicate that in a society like ours—based approvingly as it has been and is on the free marketplace (however regulated), competition, individual intiative and individual responsibility, entrepreneurship, and accumulation of money and material resources—it is inconceivable that significant sectors or groups will not have absorbed and manifested those features, individually and/or collectively. Those features are as American (United States) as apple pie, the raising of the flag on July 4, the Super Bowl, and the World Series. To assume that in their socialization psychologists have managed somehow to be exempt from the influence of these features is self-righteousness bordering on delusion. And, no less symptomatic, to act as though these same features have not crept into the substance of psychological theory contributes further to the confusion.

The question confronting psychologists is not whether these

features have crept into their theories but the ways and degrees to which they are present. This is why it is so crucial for psychology to ask where it stands in the social order and to examine the dangers that social niche poses for theory, practice, and social agentry. To ask these questions is to make social and intellectual history an essential basis for psychology. Without that basis psychology runs the risk, as it has, of being a danger and not a benefit to society. Psychologists (like the members of the manufacturers' association) are a privileged and influential group in our society. They have sought and achieved economic gains no less than they have sought and achieved influence in a wide variety of public and private institutions. Psychologists, however, have been far from sensitive to the fact that by virtue of their accomplishments they have become dependent for their incomes, status, and influence on these institutions, a fact the implications of which should not be obscured by the glib assumption that there is an identity of interests between psychologists and their clients. These implications, however, will never be pursued as long as the characteristics of the social order, its social historical development, psychology's place in that social history, and psychology's present niche in that order are not seen as core focuses for the field. These are the central issues that all the social sciences should pursue in common.

In the past few years we have seen a small but steady increase in the number of people who are casting critical eyes on the scientific enterprise, not in any nihilistic or philistine sense but in an effort either to describe more realistically the social ecology of science and the scientist or to try to make sense (in the case of social science) of sciences's failures. Mahoney (1976), Mitroff (1974, 1975), Lindblom and Cohen (1979), and Nelson (1977) are among those who have written illuminatingly along these lines. It is in no way to disparage their contributions (and the many they cite) when I say that their analyses center around the individual scientist, i.e., his or her psychology and the circumscribed milieus into which psychologists are socialized and in which they work. One comes away from reading these works with the impression that if only the scientist would face up to his or her inherent frailties and try to understand the sources of error and prejudice from within and without, the interests of science and society would be better served. This, as Mahoney (1976), a psychologist, describes and discusses so well, will require institutional and educational reforms:

> If this endeavor called "science" is indeed the noble one I consider it to be, then its continued growth and refinement is literally in your hands. It

should be obvious from the preceding chapters that I have few illusions regarding either the epistemological or psychological purities of our profession. It is a thoroughly fallible and inherently limited endeavor. Both its powers and its impotence are strikingly apparent in contemporary life. This book has focused on some of the possible sources of its dysfunction—ranging from the professional reward system to some of the absurdities in scientist training and communication.

If changes are in order—and I obviously think they are—you are their means. You may now (or soon) be in the position to exert significant impact on graduate training practices, journal publication policies, and—perhaps most critically—research priorities. With your technical skills and professional integrity, we may hope to see changes which will revolutionize both the *direction* and the *process* of science. With your sensitivity to the inequities and inhumanities which abound both inside and outside the science game, we may look toward a future of more relevant research—a future in which humanistic priorities are served by a more sensitive science. And finally, with your attitude of continual self-scrutiny and critical tentativeness, we may hopefully look forward to an era in which scientific inquiry is seen in the cautiously optimistic light of its fitting role—as a thoroughly human journey rather than some sacrosanct destination. Its challenge lies partly in its fallibility, its infinite room for refinement. Your dedicated pursuit of that endeavor has my most intense respect and encouragement. May you travel hopefully. (Pp. 175–176)

I agree with Mahoney. And, yet in the course of reading his witty but dead-serious book I found myself asking: is Mahoney aware that his description of science and scientists contains the major features of our social order? Individualism, competitiveness, the worship of technology, participation in the marketplace, adherence to "more is better" and "bigger is gorgeous"—are scientists aware that how they regard themselves and others, the theories they use to explain themselves and others, have sources in the social order and its institutions and that reforming these institutions will require more than individual resolve? Mahoney, like the others, seeks to enlarge and deepen the scientist's self-awareness as a thinking, feeling, striving social being. In a phenomenological sense that is an individual task that has built-in obstacles and limitations and chief among them is the paradox that in seeking self-understanding one must take distance from the social order and one's place in it, and yet the process of taking distance is inevitably influenced by that from which one is trying to take distance. That may be cause for being humble, but not pessimistic. There are problems that do not have complete solutions. To proceed as though that were not the case has been typically American, an ingredient in our world view that has been challenged by events of recent decades. As long as we did not have to inquire and judge our social order, as long as we felt secure about ourselves as individuals and a social order, that ingredient was axiomatic for our thinking and actions. That security is much less present. Custom and tradition have become shaky guides. A new psychology needs to be born.

There will be a new psychology but its emergence and substance cannot be predicted except in very vague outline. There is too much dissatisfaction in psychology—with its institutions, professional organizations, and directions—to expect that it can long continue in its customary ways. The fact that psychology has been catapulted, as much by the pull of world events as by the push of its own designs, into the public arena and public consciousness has affected psychology in countless ways but it has hardly changed its picture of man, which I have criticized in this book. That kind of change, I predict, will occur as more psychologists attempt to analyze and articulate the different sources of psychology's unfulfilled promise. At the very least, that kind of change will be preceded by a scrutiny of the social context out of which modern psychology emerged. That is but another way of saying that psychology will become social historical at its base. And by becoming social historical it will, willy-nilly, have to confront the nature of the society from which it sprang and how subsequent changes in the society influenced psychology's substance and cause. In short, the historical picture of psychology will deepen and change and inevitably this will change psychology's pictures of man. These pictures will no longer depict asocial, ahistorical individuals but rather contexts that have a present and a past as well as complex interconnections with larger contexts, near and far. As in all good art, these pictures will illuminate and not merely describe our realities and by this illumination help us attain a new way of seeing ourselves and our world.

In no way am I suggesting that psychology will or should become history but rather that psychologists will conceptualize social structure, social order, and social history in ways that will drastically alter how they conceptualize and literally see human behavior, their own as well as that of others. They will see themselves and others as historical beings but not historical in a narrow, intrapsychic sense, which assigns the social structure to a very secondary status. Psychology will assume a historical stance that will be a basis for looking back and finding it surprising that the psychology of a John Dewey, a J. F. Brown, a Thomas Gladwin, or a John Dollard was met with silence and incomprehension when it was met at all. These writers will be honored not because they said it all (they did not) or because they were so right in details and prediction (they were not) but because they saw more clearly than did their peers that customary and traditional psychology has to be transcended and replaced. They had the courage and vision (literally and metaphorically) to try to see things whole. Too often "to see things whole" is a phrase used as a badge of honor but so empty of meaning that one concludes that "deep down he is shallow." These writers plumbed depths that we would do well to comprehend.

Make no mistake about it, the task of understanding the social historical origins of modern psychology will not be an easy one, if only because the psychologist will have to recognize and control for biases that are a consequence of his or her own socialization. Once this issue surfaces in psychology it will signify that psychology's world view has changed, and one of the consequences will be (I hope) that psychology will come to value understanding and to deemphasize the role of measurement. Psychology has for too long sought to measure a world of its own contrivance, and this it has done extremely well—so well that for decades it did not have to face the possibility that ingeniously measuring a world of one's own making is a mammoth waste of time. In its own way psychology committed itself to the cult of standardization, i.e., to contrive situations that would be standard for all people. This seemed to meet the scientific requirements of objectivity, reliability, and validity but at the expense of recognizing or pursuing the following question: how does behavior in standardized situations relate to and illuminate behavior in naturally occurring situations?

When a new psychology emerges it will not be because of formal research and new data, although these will play a role. Rather, it will be because of changes in world view that will take place as generations of new psychologists are socialized into a national and international order dramatically different from that of the post–World War II era. Past generations of psychologists dealt with the nature and structure of the human mind. *That* was what fascinated them. Coming generations will find themselves, I predict, no less fascinated with the nature and structure of social orders, their own and others, because so much of their daily experience will be suffused for good or for bad with changes and clashes within and among the social orders this world contains. One does not have to worry about any lessening in fascination, among psychologists and people generally, with the nature and structure of the human mind. One does have to worry about how these changes and clashes will help create a new psychology. The present is pregnant with many futures and not all of them are pleasant to contemplate. But our task is less to contemplate these futures and more to try to understand how they have come to be possibilities. The effort to understand where we are going presupposes that we know how we got where we are. This kind of understanding is distinctive by its absence in psychology. If I am right, this kind of understanding is what psychologists, in their professional and personal lives, are beginning to want to seek.

BIBLIOGRAPHY

ALLPORT, G. *Personality: A Psychological Interpretation.* New York: Holt, 1937.

———. "The Psychologist's Frame of Reference." In E. Hilgard (ed.), *American Psychology in Historical Perspective.* Washington, D.C.: American Psychological Association, 1978.

BECKER, E. *The Lost Science of Man.* New York: Braziller, 1971.

BENDIX, R., and LIPSET, S. M. *Class, Status, and Power.* New York: Free Press, 1953.

BERKOWITZ, L. "Theoretical and Research Approaches in Experimental Social Psychology." In A. R. Gelgen, (ed.), *Contemporary Scientific Psychology.* New York: Academic Press, 1970.

BINET, A., and SIMON, T. *The Development of Intelligence in Children.* Trans. Elizabeth S. Kite. Baltimore: Williams & Wilkins, 1916. (a)

———. *The Intelligence of the Feebleminded.* Trans. Elizabeth S. Kite. Baltimore: Williams & Wilkins, 1916. (b)

BROWN, J. F. *Psychology and the Social Order.* New York: McGraw-Hill, 1936.

CANCE, A. E., FIELD, J. A., WARD, R. D., and HALL, P. F. "First Report of the Committee on Emigration of the Eugenics Section." *American Breeders Magazine* (1912) 3:249–255.

CATTELL, J. M. "The Progress of Psychology as an Experimental Science." In E. Hilgard (ed.), *American Psychology in Historical Perspective.* Washington, D.C.: American Psychological Association, 1978.

COLE, M., et al. *Ecological Niche Picking: Ecological Invalidity as an Axiom of Experimental Cognitive Psychology.* New York: Rockefeller University, Laboratory of Comparative Human Cognition and Institute for Comparative Human Development (undated).

———. *What's Cultural About Cross-cultural Cognitive Psychology?* New York: Rockefeller University, Laboratory of Comparative Human Cognition and Institute for Comparative Human Development (undated).

———. *Cognition as a Residual Category in Anthropology*. New York: Rockefeller University, Laboratory of Comparative Human Cognition and Institute for Comparative Human Development (undated).

DAVIS, A. *Social-Class Influences upon Learning*. Cambridge: Harvard University Press, 1951.

DEWEY, J. *The Quest for Certainty*. New York: Putnam, 1960 (paperback).

———. "Psychology and Social Practice." In E. Hilgard (ed.), *American Psychology in Historical Perspective*. Washington, D.C.: American Psychological Association, 1978.

DOLLARD, J. *Criteria for the Life History*. New Haven: Yale University Press, 1935.

DOLLARD, J., DOOB, L., MILLER, N., MOWRER, O. H., AND SEARS, R. *Frustration and Aggression*. New Haven: Yale University Press, 1939.

DOOB, L. W. "The Utilization of Social Scientists in the Overseas Branch of the Office of War Information." *American Political Science Review* (1947) 41(no. 4): 649–677.

FREUD, S. In P. Friedman (ed.), *On Suicide: Discussions of the Vienna Psychoanalytic Society, 1910*. New York: International Universities Press, 1967.

GALBRAITH, J. K. Introduction to Thorstein Veblen, *The Theory of the Leisure Class*. Boston: Houghton Mifflin, 1973.

GALTON, F. *Hereditary Genius*. London: Macmillan, 1869.

GARNER, W. "The Acquisition and Application of Knowledge." *American Psychologist* (1972), 27(no. 10):941–946.

GERGEN, K. J. "Social Psychology as History." *Journal of Personality and Social Psychology* (1973) 26(no. 2):309–320.

———. "Social Psychology, Science, and History." *Personality and Social Psychology Bulletin* (1976) 2:373–383.

———. "Experimentation in Social Psychology: A Reappraisal." *European Journal of Social Psychology* (1978) 8:507–527.

———. "The Positivist Image in Social Psychological Theory." In A. R. Buss (ed.), *Psychology in Social Context*. New York: Irvington, 1979. (a)

———. "Social Psychology and the Phoenix of Unreality." Address given at the Centennial Symposium of the annual meeting of the American Psychological Association, New York City, 1979. (b)

GLADWIN, T. *Slaves of the white myth: The Psychology of Neocolonialism*. Atlantic Highlands, N.J.: Humanities Press, 1980.

GODDARD, H. H. "The Binet Tests in Relation to Immigration." *Journal of Psychoasthenics* (1913) 18:105–110.

———. "Mental Tests and the Immigrant." *Journal of Delinquency* (1917) 2:243–277.

GOULD, R. A. *Yiwara: Foragers of the Australian Desert*. New York: Scribner's, 1969.

GOULDNER, A. *The Coming Crisis of Western Sociology*. New York: Basic Books, 1970.

HALLER, M. *Eugenics: Hereditarian Attitudes in American Thought*. New Brunswick: Rutgers University Press, 1963.

HEILBRONNER, R. *The Worldly Philosophers*. New York: Simon & Schuster, 1961.

HERRNSTEIN, R. J. *I. Q. in the Meritocracy*. Boston: Little, Brown, 1973.

HILGARD, E. (ed.), *American Psychology in Historical Perspective: Addresses of the Presidents of the American Psychological Association, 1892–1977*. Washington, D.C.: American Psychological Association, 1978.

HOFSTADTER, R. *Social Darwinism in American Thought.* Rev. ed. New York: Braziller, 1959.

JAMES, W. *Essays in Radical Empiricism.* New York: Dutton, 1971.

———. "The Knowing of Things Together." In E. Hilgard (ed.), *American Psychology in Historical Persepective.* Washington, D.C.: American Psychological Association, 1978.

KAMIN, I. J., *The Science and Politics of I.Q.* Hillsdale: Lawrence Erlbaum Associates, 1974.

KATZ, D. "Some Final Considerations about Experimentation in Social Psychology." In C. G. McClintock (ed.), *Experimental Social Psychology.* New York: Holt, Rinehart & Winston, 1972.

KESSEN, W. "The American Child and Other Cultural Inventions." *American Psychologist* (1979) 34(no. 10):815–820.

KOYRE, A. *Newtonian Studies.* Chicago: University of Chicago Press, 1965.

LINDBLOM, C. E., AND COHEN, D. K. *Usable Knowledge.* New Haven: Yale University Press, 1979.

MAHONEY, M. J. *Scientist as Subject: The Psychological Imperative.* Cambridge: Ballinger, 1976.

MILLS, C. W. *The Sociological Imagination.* New York: Oxford University Press, 1959.

MITROFF, J. J. "Norms and Counter-norms in a Select Group of the Apollo Scientists: A Case Study of the Ambivalence of Scientists." *American Sociological Review* (1975) 39:579–595. (a)

———. *The Subjective Side of Science.* New York: Elsevier, 1974. (b)

MURRAY, H. A. *Explorations in Personality.* New York: Oxford University Press, 1938.

NELSON, R. *The Moon and the Ghetto.* New York: Norton, 1977.

NISBET, R. *The Degradation of the Academic Dogma.* New York: Basic Books, 1971. (a)

———. *The Quest for Community.* New York: Oxford University Press, 1971. (b)

———. *The Social Philosophers.* New York: Crowell, 1973.

OSBORN, H. F. In M. Grant. *The Passing of the Great Race.* New York: Scribner's, 1919. (Preface to revised edition, 1917).

PROSHANSKY, H. M. "For What Are We Training Our Graduate Students?" *American Psychologist* (1972) 27:205–212.

———. "Applications of Social Psychology: Conceptions and Misconceptions." In K. Salzinger and F. L. Denmark (eds.), *Psychology: The State of rht Art.* New York: New York Academy of Sciences, 1978.

SARASON, S. B. *Psychological Problems in Mental Deficiency.* 3d ed. New York: Harper, 1959. First published 1949.

———. *The Culture of the School and the Problem of Change.* Boston: Allyn & Bacon, 1971.

———. *The Creation of Settings and the Future Societies.* San Francisco: Jossey-Bass, 1972.

———. "Psychology to the Finland Station in the Heavenly City of the Eighteenth Century Philosophers." *American Psychologist* (1975) 30(no. 11):1072–1080.

———. *Work, Aging, and Social Change: Professionals and the One Life–One Career Imperative.* New York: Free Press, 1977.

———. "Individual Psychology: An Obstacle to Comprehending Adulthood." In L. A. Bond and J. C. Rosen (eds.), *Competence and Coping during Adulthood.* Hanover: University Press of New England, 1980.

SARASON, S. B. and DORIS, J. *Psychological Problems in Mental Deficiency.* 4th ed. New York: Harper & Row, 1969.

———. *Educational Handicap, Public Policy, and Social History: A Broadened Perspective on Mental Retardation.* New York: Free Press, 1979.

SARASON, S. B., AND GLADWIN, T. "Psychological and Cultural Problems in Mental Subnormality: A Review of Research." *Genetic Psychology Monographs* (1958) 57:3–290.

SCARR, S. "From Evaluation to Larry P., or What Shall We Do about I.Q. Tests?" *Intelligence,* (1978) 2:325–342.

SCHAFER, R. "The Idea of Resistance." *International Journal of Psycho-Analysis* (1973) 54:259–283.

SKINNER, B. F. *Walden Two.* New York: Macmillan, 1972 (paperback).

SMITH, B. "Is Psychology Relevant to New Priorities?" *American Psychologist* (1973) 28:463–471.

SPOCK, B. *Baby and Child Care.* New York: Pocket Books, 1945.

THORNDIKE, E. L. *Human Nature and the Social Order.* Abr. ed. Cambridge: MIT Press, 1969.

VEBLEN, T. *The Higher Learning in America: A Memorandum on the Conduct of Universities by Businessmen.* New York: Sagamore, 1957.

———. *The Theory of the Leisure Class.* Boston: Houghton Mifflin, 1973.

WARNER, L. *Yankee City.* Abr. ed. New Haven: Yale University Press, 1964.

WOLF, T. *Alfred Binet.* Chicago: University of Chicago Press, 1973.

YERKES, R. M. "Psychology in Relation to the War." In E. Hilgard (ed.), *American Psychology in Historical Perspective.* Washington, D.C.: American Psychological Association, 1978.